Islam

Text copyright © 2016 remains with the authors and for the collection with ATF Theology. All rights reserved. Except for any fair dealing permitted under the Copyright Act, no part of the publication may be reproduced by any means without prior permission. Inquiries should be made in the first instance with the publisher.

A Forum for Theology in the World
Volume 3, Issue 1, 2016

A Forum for Theology in the World is an academic refereed journal aimed at engaging with issues in the contemporary world, a world which is pluralist and eucumenical in nature. The journal reflects this pluralism and ecumenism. Each edition is theme specific and has its own editor responsible for the production. The journal aims to elicit and encourage dialogue on topics and issues in contemporary society and within a variety of religious traditions. The Editor in Chief welcomes submissions of manuscripts, collections of articles, for review from individuals or institutions, which may be from seminars or conferences or written specifically for the journal. An internal peer review is expected before submitting the manuscript. It is the expectation of the publisher that, once a manuscript has been accepted for publication, it will be submitted according to the house style to be found at the back of this volume. All submissions to the Editor in Chief are to be sent to: hdregan@atf.org.au.

Each edition is available as a journal subscription, or as a book in print, pdf or epub, through the ATF Press web site — www.atfpress.com. Journal subscriptions are also available through EBSCO and other library suppliers.

Editor in Chief
Hilary Regan, ATF Press

A Forum for Theology in the World is published by ATF Theology and imprint of
ATF (Australia) Ltd (ABN 90 116 359 963) and
is published twice or three times a year.
ISSN 1329-6264

ATF Press
PO Box 504
Hindmarsh SA 5007
Australia
www.atfpress.com

Subscription Rates 2016

Print	On-Line	Print and On-line
Aust $65 Individuals	Aus $55 individuals	Aus $75 individuals
Aus $90 Institutions	Aus $80 individuals	Aus $100 instiutions

Islam
Its Beginnings and History, Its Theology and Its Importance Today

Robert Crotty and Terence Lovat

ATF Theology
Adelaide
2016

Forum for Theology in the World Vol 3 No 1/2016

A Note to the Reader

This book is based on the research of the authors completed over many years. In turn, this research draws on the research of many other scholars who have addressed various aspects of the topic. In that sense, the book is a scholarly one, but we have chosen to make it as accessible as possible to a wide audience and so did not want to burden the text with too many references and footnotes. These are mainly left to a separate section at the end of each chapter and then the bibliography at the end of the book is intended for those readers who wish to follow up on one or other aspect of the text.

Please note also that we, the same two authors, have recently published a more intensive version of our research around the same topic. This book is titled *Reconciling Islam, Christianity and Judaism: Islam's Special Role in Restoring Convivencia,* published in 2015 by Springer Press, Heidelberg, Germany.

Terence Lovat
Robert Crotty

Preface

Terrorism is the threat of the age, or so we are told. The threat, at least as much as the reality, has at times ruined airline companies and tourist operators, thrown national economies into disarray and caused corporate collapse around the globe. The spectre of '9/11', Bali, Baghdad, Madrid, London, Glasgow, Boston, Sydney, Paris, Tunis, Chad, Bangkok, Basra and Palmyra confronts us daily and nightly through our media. Reports from airlines tell us that it takes no more than a minor scare at an airport anywhere in the world to cause cancellations of seats and even flights. In the face of rational comment and any amount of evidence about the far greater threat to the world of AIDS, TB, malaria, asthma, obesity and malnutrition, it is terrorism nonetheless that has the focal attention of the world and its media.

Behind the grip of terrorism lies the word, 'Islam'. The notion of the 'Muslim terrorist' has become a colloquialism in Western media. Interestingly, in all the history books and commentaries about the Second World War in Europe, the fascism and anti-Semitism on which the Nazi Third Reich was built is rarely if ever coupled with the word 'Christian', in spite of the fact that the Third Reich made carefully constructed use of age-old Christian biases and pseudo-theologies, just as some modern terrorism employs Islamic equivalents. The same case could be made about the Ku Klux Klan, the IRA, the South African apartheid advocates, or any number of other such instances where the perpetrators claimed their actions to be based somehow on their Christian beliefs.

Perhaps the reason that Westerners do not do to Christians the same injustice that we do to Muslims relates to our being at least slightly better informed about Christianity, if not altogether sympathetic to it, and about its many complexities and differences. Through greater understanding, our facility to generalise and stereotype is slowed. Moreover, even in what is largely a post-church age, we seem to have too great a regard for Christianity and its principles than to allow its image to be polluted so easily by the claims of those whom we see clearly to be functioning outside of its norms and codes of conduct. Additionally, it could be that we are simply too sensitive to the feelings of those who align with Christianity to risk offending them. If these explanations come close to uncovering the reasons for the difference between the ways in which we ascribe a religious cause for terrorism to Christianity and Islam, then the challenge for restoring justice to Islam would seem to be for formal and informal education to take the goal of enhanced literacy about Islam more seriously.

We need to achieve the same understanding about Islam that seems implicit about the understanding of Christianity, namely: that it is complex and different within itself, and so cannot be generalised about and stereotyped; that it has a set of principles, norms and a code of conduct that makes terrorism as incongruous to it as terrorism is incongruous to Christianity; and, that its followers are as liable to be offended, hurt and confused when their religion is so easily associated with terrorism as Christians would be if Christianity was routinely referred to in the same way.

Not that this is to suggest that Islam as a whole can be exonerated from its association with terrorism any more than Christianity can be exonerated from its role in the Crusades or the IRA, or Judaism from recent events in Palestine. What can be said is that Islam plays some part. In reality, it may be a minor, largely *prima facie* part, and most Muslims will rightly claim that it is a perverted form of Islam that plays a part in terrorism at that. Nonetheless, it is undeniable that the perpetrators of 9/11, Bali, Paris and Tunis, as just a few among many instances, claimed to be motivated by their Islamic beliefs and values. How is this so? How can a religion with such strong injunctions towards the establishment of peace, social justice and the acceptance of people of other beliefs end up being exploited in this way?

An easy answer may be that these perpetrators are just fanatics or, a little more helpfully perhaps, that they do not truly know and understand Islam other than in some aberrant way. Granted that education in many Muslim countries does not function well, and furthermore that religious education in Muslim and many non-Muslim countries is often in the hands of local officials and volunteers with their own fairly narrow and fundamentalist understanding of Islam and/or political agendas, it is easy to see how people could come to believe all sorts of things that the scholar of Islam would not recognise.

The easy explanations that terrorists are either fanatics or poorly educated is confounded, of course, when one finds well-informed, and even scholarly people claiming to be Muslim taking up with a terrorist cause. It is easy enough to explain how a young, relatively uneducated and socially deprived zealot gets caught up with a cause leading to destruction, but what about an apparently well-trained cleric or an imam (official interpreter of the Qur'an) or a Western-trained medical doctor (as happened in Glasgow) or an aspiring medical student in a top US university (as happened in Boston)? What are we dealing with when a young man in good social circumstances, a young family, with apparently much to live for, a history of care and compassion especially for children, straps on a bomb and blows himself up together with a bevy of innocents including young children? What do we say when the bomber is a woman or a child? In cases like this, the easy answer becomes less easy. This is where the history of Islam, including its relationship with Judaism and Christianity in the West, and its current socio-cultural circumstances becomes relevant.

The purpose of this book is to address some of these issues and to restore some balance in our understanding of Islam. This will be done through exploring briefly the essence of its theology, elements of which are close to the theologies of Christianity and Judaism, as well as overviewing its remarkable achievements and contributions to science and civilised living, especially in medieval times. It will focus on the often-termed 'Golden Age of Islam' for the scientific, cultural and welfare achievements that influenced Western development so markedly in these same areas, as well as Islam's unique role in establishing some of the most tolerant multicultural and multi-faith civilisations ever known, including most particularly its tolerance towards Jews and Christians.

The book sets out therefore to recover some justice for Islam by confronting and contradicting those ideas that make Islam out to be fundamentally at odds with the West. Our perspective is very much about Islam as part of the Western story and about Islam's own Middle Eastern origins. Our perspective is directed towards Islam as a sibling religion of Judaism and Christianity and as one that has huge potential to inform its siblings about their own origins and medieval development, as well as the development of Western civilisation generally.

Of course, we do not retreat from the reality that Islam is regarded widely in very different ways, particularly in the West, and we will attempt to uncover the causes and the ensuing troubling theologies that threaten to turn Islam into the very thing that so many people fear about it.

Above all, however, we want to paint a picture of Islam as an indispensable part of what most Westerners take for granted. Be it about modern medicine, science, education, social welfare, the role of women, of family, of human rights or of social justice, had there been no Islam, we quite likely would not be where we are today. The fact that so few Westerners recognise this is one of the tragic gaps in our education and self-understanding. The fact that, in all likelihood, so few Muslims understand these achievements is also part of the problem we are addressing.

Finally, we offer a word of caution that, while there are some clear commonalities in the phenomenon we know as 'Islam', there are also many differences in the worldwide groups and communities that go by the name. Just as Christianity has its Orthodox, Catholic and Protestant forms, with vast differences within each, the same is true of Islam, arguably even more so. The caution is therefore about over-generalising and, especially stereotyping. With Islam, we are dealing with difference, too much difference to be able to do justice to in a book this size. The book therefore will generalise, but hopefully not stereotype. We generalise with caution and advise the reader to do the same. The only way to really know about any Islamic group is to get to know that group and especially the individuals within it, a good thing to do anyway.

Notes

As mentioned in the Note to Readers, a more extended version of this book, which readers may wish to consult, has already been published as:

> Lovat, T & Crotty, R (2015). *Reconciling Islam, Christianity and Judaism: Islam's special role in restoring Convivencia*. Heidelberg, Germany: Springer.

On the role of education and interfaith understanding in the whole question of the Abrahamic religions see:

> Lovat, T (2005). Educating about Islam and learning about self: An approach for our times. *Religious Education, 100,* 38-51.
> Lovat, T (2006). Islam as the religion of 'fair go': An important lesson for Australian religious education. *Journal of Religious Education, 54,* 49-53.
> Lovat, T (2010). Improving relations with Islam through religious and values education. In K Engebretson, M de Souza, G Durka & L Gearon (Eds), *International handbook of inter-religious education* (pp 695-708). New York: Springer.
> Lovat, T (2012). Interfaith education and phenomenological method. In T van der Zee & T Lovat (Eds), *New perspectives on religious and spiritual education* (pp 87-100). Munster: Waxmann.
> Lovat, T, Clement, N, Dally, K & Toomey, R (2010). Addressing issues of religious difference through values education: An Islam instance. *Cambridge Journal of Education, 40,* 213-227.

Forum for Theology in the World Vol 3 No 1/2016

Contents

Preface	vii
1. Introduction	xv
2. Early History of the Arabs	1
3. The Message of Islam	11
4. The Beginnings of Islam and the Prophet Muhammad	17
5. The Qur'an as a Source of Truth for Islamic Thought and Practice	41
6. The Sunnah of Muhammad	49
7. The Five Pillars of Islam	55
8. The Early Divisions of Islam	61
9. Later Islamic History and More Divisions	71
10. Distinctive Features of the Ummah of Islam	79
11. Recovering Early Principles and Reforms: An Interpretation	87
12. Medieval Reform and Scholarship	97
13. Islam and the Wider Christian and Jewish Relationship	105
14. The Muslim Jesus	119
15. A Story of Loss and the Beginnings of the Troubles we still deal with Today	123
16. Conclusion	131
Bibliography	135

1
Introduction

Islam is a religion of enormous proportions in our world. At the last attempt at a census (in 2012), it was estimated that there are 1.57 billion Muslims across the globe. This was 23% of the total world population at the time. There are forty-nine countries where Islam is the dominant religion. The largest concentrations are in the Middle East, Africa and North Africa, as well as parts of Asia. The largest Muslim population in any one country is in Indonesia, 87.2% of whose people profess to be Muslims. Indonesia alone accounts for 12.7% of the total Muslim population of the world.

There is much research yet to be done on precisely when and where the religion called 'Islam' actually formed as a distinct religious movement. The fifth to ninth centuries in the Middle East saw a multitude of religious movements claiming to be following the 'One True God'. The dominant interpretation however is that Islam began during the seventh century CE (or the first century of the Muslim calendar) in the western section of what is today Saudi Arabia. The word *islam* in Arabic means 'submission' and this describes the basic attitude and central posturing of the religion—it is a religion about submission to the one true God, named *Allah*, Arabic for 'The God'. A follower of Islam is therefore a *muslim*, meaning a 'submitted one'. Submission describes the fundamental religious attitude and positioning of one who follows the religion established by the founder, Muhammad, an Arabic name that means 'the praiseworthy one'.

Of major importance, as well as a point of contention concerning which much more will be said later in this book, the dominant story suggests that the central character, Muhammad, did not consider himself to be establishing a new religion, but rather to be restoring a very ancient one and bringing it to completion. This gives us a vital clue about the role of Islam in the history of religions, and especially the so-called 'Abrahamic religions' of Judaism, Christianity and Islam.

There are a number of divisions in the total Islamic population. The most numerous belong to the broad category known as Sunni Islam, accounting for some 75-90% of the Islamic peoples, with the other major category being Shia Islam, accounting for some 10-20% of the total Muslim population. As suggested, these are just the broad categories with a myriad of sub-categories within each one. Arguably, there are more divisions and species of Islam than of any other religion that has ever existed. Again, it needs to be said, this gives us a vital clue about why it is so impossible to generalise about and, least of all, stereotype Islam and also why it is so difficult for any one individual or group to speak for Islam as a whole, though many would like to think they can.

The statistics above offer good reasons for non-Muslims (for whom this book is primarily, though not exclusively, intended) to study and understand Islam. It is a dominant force in the world and it takes many forms, most of them as unknown to fellow Muslims as they are to non-Muslims. More importantly, we are assured that Islam will play an increasingly greater role in world history. It is predicted, for example, that the world's Muslim population is increasing at twice the rate of non-Muslims (Pew Research Center, 2011). This is being achieved both by rapid conversion and superior reproduction. Statistics suggest that more religionists are attracted to its core beliefs and style of living than to any other form of religion and, additionally, that Muslims are having more children than the followers of any other religion or, indeed, than those who follow no religion. It has been estimated that, by 2100, if these trends continue, there will be more Muslims than Christians in the world (Pew Research Center, 2011).

Islam is a religion. It has a world-wide following. Most countries of the world, despite the fact that they have a majority non-Muslim population, are being faced with the reality of Muslim immigration and so the reality of an emerging Muslim culture and its associated Islamic religion. In Western Europe, for example, some 6% of the population is now Muslim. In Eastern Europe, the proportion is even greater.[1] This fact is often alleged to be creating more and more social problems in Europe. How can Muslims and non-Muslims live side by side in the same geographical space? These facts of immigration and expansion have caused the Western world only recently to begin developing a more realistic image of Islam in world history. For instance, there is an awakening in the West to the achievements of Islam: in art, architecture and ceramics; in literature of many kinds; in philosophy, at times far more advanced than the Europeans, including in the integration of the great Greek philosophers of ancient times; in the sciences, including medicine, and technology.

Today, Islam is experiencing resurgence, a rediscovering of its own rich social and religious heritage, as well as its intellectual achievements. Its vitality is marked by a modern missionary expansion, especially in Africa and Asia. It is vital therefore that Western populations extend on their fairly poor knowledge of Islam. In that context, this book represents an attempt to assist in that task. We begin with some of the important history that sits behind the emergence of Islam.

Notes

A handy compendium of statistics on modern Islam, as used in the above text, can be found in:

> Pew Research Center (2011). The future of the global Muslim population. *Pew Research Center: Religion and Public Life.* Available at: http://www.pewforum.org/2011/01/27/the-future-of-the-global-muslim-population/

---

1. Eastern Europe numbers about 44 million Muslims, with some countries having a majority Muslim population. Turkey's population is nearly 99% Muslim, some 74 million people.

2
Early History of the Arabs

A religion does not begin in a vacuum. It is necessary to study its particular social, cultural and even political setting. In the case of Islam, it is essential to recall that its ancient origins were well before the 600s CE and the events associated with the character known as Muhammad. Islamic tradition itself claims that its real beginnings should be traced to the time of Ibrahim (known by Jews and Christians as Abraham), regarded by Muslims as the first monotheist and an Arab. By this same interpretation, all the major Prophets, from Adam, the first human, to Jesus, were Muslims.[1]

The role of Muhammad can only be understood in this context: he was the last and the greatest of the Prophets, sent to complete the revelation of the religion that had begun with Ibrahim. We will see that this Muslim claim is of great interest, not least in the context of current world events, even if its historical justification is, as with most religion's foundational stories, more about legend than history in the modern social science sense.

---

1. Islam counts 25 prophets from Adam to Jesus, although it mentions that there were others not named in its texts.

Origin of the Arabs

We can begin with the background of Arabs in the ancient Middle East in the millennium before the advent of Christianity. The first record of the use of 'Arab' (to describe a person) occurred in the ninth century BCE. This was on an Akkadian inscription dealing with the conquest of Syria by the Assyrians (Retsö, 2003). The Assyrians were opposed by a coalition which they defeated. As a result, the Assyrian king took booty from the coalition, including one thousand camels from Gindibu the Arab (*ar-ba-a-a*).

Who was Gindibu? He seems to have been a rebellious prince. What did *ar-ba-a-a* mean? This is more difficult. Scholars have tried to explain it in several ways: 'Arab' has been said to come from the word *gharab* or 'West' because the Arabs had originated from the west of Mesopotamia; 'Arab' has been said to come from the name of the ancient Arabah valley, and the Ishmaelites who lived there were called 'Arabs'; 'Arab' has been said to come from *arava* or 'wilderness' because they were desert people.

Despite our lack of knowledge about the name 'Arab', in the ninth century BCE, we seem to be dealing with a tribal people who lived in the Arabian Peninsula, a huge expanse of some two million square kilometres. They would have been nomads and semi-nomads, tribespeople within the interminable wastelands. They would have come under the broad control first of the Egyptians (during the New Kingdom 1570-1070 BCE, and then sporadically during the third Intermediate period 1070-664 BCE), the Assyrians (911-605 BCE), the Babylonians (605-539 BCE), the Persians (539-332 BCE), the Seleucid Greeks (312-63 BCE) and the Roman Empire (from the first century BCE onwards).

The Birth of Arab Civilisations

In the Christian era, the Parthians from Iran came to dominate Arab life. These latter people had come to power in north-east Iran and, after 227 BCE, they managed to take over most of Iran and establish their own Empire. From their base, they made frequent incursions into the Middle East. However, frequent wars with the Romans and with nomadic tribes took their toll and the Empire fractured and the Persians overcame the Parthians in 224 CE. The Arabs lived on the fringes of these societies and continued their semi-nomadic way of life, sometimes with difficulty.

The Arabs spread far into the Arabian Peninsula, known as such for that very reason. In the south of the Peninsula, a large dam had been constructed around 750 BCE and, as a result of increased agriculture, trade had flourished. The Arabs produced cereals, myrrh, incense and spices. As they settled down and gave up their nomadic existence, they were ruled by kings in a line of succession and the kings were known as *mukarrib* or 'sacrificers'. Their religion was polytheistic and they had a basic system of temples and a priesthood to assist the king. Kings and priests offered sacrifices to their gods. The priests were called *kahins* (or 'seer'; later, Jews would use a similar word, *kohen*, for priest). They acted as custodians of the sacred sanctuaries and ensured that the proper rituals were carried out. They were also believed to be able to foretell the future. These *kahins* were considered by the tribe to have special powers to see and hear things that others could not. Under the inspiration of a god, they chanted in rhyme and communicated what they had experienced. They were listened to with awe and reverence.

In the north of the Arabian Peninsula, there was a more tribal system, known today as Bedouin tribalism. The social unit was the tribe and the members were committed to self-defence of the tribe and tracing blood descent within the tribe was considered obligatory.

There were collective rights among the Arabs to water, pastures and animals. Their religion was polydaemonism, whereby divinity was perceived to reside in trees, water sources and sacred stones. These objects became symbols that represented the spiritual powers inhabiting their world. The nomads carried with them a symbol of their main tribal god, usually in the form of a sacred stone housed in a red tent.

As the Arabs settled, they established towns. One was Mecca, founded by a northern tribe, the Quraysh, on the trade route from the south up to the Middle East and on an earlier site which had been a centre for Arab worship. The Quraysh were actually a consortium of Arab tribes. While each tribe maintained its own identity, there was much in common—culture, practices, beliefs—among the consortium.

So, in Mecca, sacred symbols were collected in a cubic shrine, the *Ka'aba* or 'Cube', which still stands today. It was believed that the Ka'aba had predated the actual establishment of the city of Mecca. The symbols were the totems of tribes that lived in the surrounds and they had been placed there prior to that construction. Because of this possession of the Ka'aba, the Quraysh were regarded by other tribal groupings as being more prestigious. They were the custodians of the many gods of the tribes; any talk of only one god would not have been welcome in their midst. Another town established in a similar way was at an oasis further north, Yathrib. According to the dominant story, both these towns would become vital to the beginnings of Islam.

The Arabs in the Arabian Peninsula began to spread during the early Christian centuries. There was tribal movement from the Arabian Peninsula into South Syria and the southern section of Jordan from about the middle of the third century CE. These Arabs brought with them Arab culture and the Arab language and they found Arabs like themselves in the areas that were developed there.

Confronting Romans and Christians

The Arabs also confronted the Romans. The area later called Palestine had been first ruled, after the time of the world empire established by Alexander the Great in the fourth century BCE, by his successors, the Ptolemies in Egypt for a short time and then the Seleucids. The Seleucids were Greeks who ruled the local populations in what we would today call Jordan, Israel, Syria, etc. The people in Judah, the area around Jerusalem, had rallied their forces, led by a family known as the Maccabees. These warrior chieftains had managed to set up their own kingdom with Jerusalem at its centre. The ruling family became known as the Hasmoneans.

This brief assertion of authority on the part of the Hasmoneans, broadly between 165 BCE and 63 BCE, was halted by the arrival of the Romans in the East. The Romans, under Pompey the Great, took over the Hasmonean possessions in 63 BCE. From that time, they would be the rulers until the time of Islam in the seventh century CE. The Jews revolted during the first and second centuries CE but were harshly put down. Jerusalem was destroyed and would only be rebuilt under the Roman Emperor, Hadrian, as a Roman city called Aelia Capitolina in the years after 130 CE.

In the fourth century CE, Constantine the Great unexpectedly announced that Christianity would be accorded the standing of a legitimate religion in the Roman Empire—a *religio licita*. During his time, great monuments were erected in Palestine on the sites of Jesus' birth, crucifixion, burial and ascension.

Constantine made another momentous decision. He moved the capital of the Empire from Rome to Constantinople. There were strategic and military reasons for this move. He intended it to be New Rome cutting ties with the earlier bureaucracy in Rome.

One of his successors, Theodosius I, went further than Constantine had done in the religious sphere and made Christianity the formal religion of the Roman Empire.

This was the world in which the Arabs from the Arabian Peninsula found themselves involved. Some of them became Christians, such as the Ghassanids, the Lakhmids and the Banu Judham, while many Arabs had been Christians from the earliest days of Christianity. We know for instance that there was a thriving Christian community in Mecca from about 150 CE, that some of the earliest Christian monastics were Arabic and that, by 300 CE, one of the largest and most important Christian centres was in Alexandria in Egypt and that the first great Council of the church was held at Nicaea in what is now Turkey.

We also know that early important Christian figures, like the Patriarchs Alexander and Athanasius, the great theologian, Augustine of Hippo, and indeed the alleged heretic, Arius, were all of Arabic stock. Philip Jenkins (2009) says of Arabic Christianity that it forms a largely 'lost Christianity', partly because it 'lost out' to the dominant Western church in some of the early Christological disputes about the nature of Christ as part of the Trinity. By 451 CE (the year of the Council of Chalcedon), the Coptic (Egyptian) Orthodox Church had formally split with the rest of the church, Western and Eastern.

Many of these disenfranchised Arabic Christians would, a couple of centuries later, be among the first converts to Islam. Granted their history, they would likely have seen Islam as both an improved version of the Abrahamic tradition as well as having a closer understanding of Jesus than mainstream Christianity which they would have regarded as heretical, most especially in its Western Roman form. Other Arabic Christians would remain Christian but would go on to feel very comfortable living as Christians with their fellow Abrahamic followers, the Muslims, more commonly known in Islam's early days as Ishmaelites, Hagarians and, later, Saracens.

As mentioned, many more Arabs became Christians as a result of the incursions mentioned above. The Ghassanids had moved from the Arabian Peninsula in the third century CE into the Levant. After settling there, they easily merged into Greek Christian society. They became a client state of the Romans and fought with them against the Persian Sassanids. The Romans found that their lands were handy as a buffer zone against raids by Arab Bedouins.

The Lakhmids were an Arab tribe which had moved from the south of the Arabian Peninsula, now Yemen, and settled to the south of Iraq in a capital called al-Hirah in the third century CE. They were defeated by the Persians in the next century. The Banu Judham were also from the south Arabian area but migrated to Syria and Egypt. They lived comfortably within the Ghassanid Empire and were described as a Christian tribe. They eventually became a confederation within the Byzantine Empire.

As suggested, later on, many of these Christians would convert to Islam. This process of conversion and assimilation between Muslims, Christians and Jews would continue for centuries, most obviously and successfully in the great cities and towns of Moorish Spain between 711 and 1492 CE, the era we refer to, following the Spanish usage, as *Convivencia* or harmonious co-existence (Lovat & Crotty, 2015). This assimilation and co-existence was facilitated by the work of Muhammad al-Tabari (1990) who constructed in the 800s CE a 'history' that placed Islam at the centre of God's plan for the world but also paid due regard to the role of Judaism and Christianity in the evolution of that plan. Theologically, this is what justified Muslims regarding Jews and Christians as fellow religionists and 'Peoples of the Book', about which more will be said later.

Tabari's work in many ways represents the conceptual beginnings of Islam as a unified movement but it was preceded by various Arab movements and incursions in the centuries beforehand, many of them amounting to earlier Muslim manifestations.

This Arab movement out of the Arabian Peninsula northwards meant that the tribes were gradually assimilated into larger groups. In fact, by the seventh and eighth century CE, the early beginnings of Islam, Arabs as such would have had little effect on the world scene since they had been absorbed into so many larger groups.

Using modern geographical terms, before the seventh to eighth centuries CE, Lebanon and Syria would only have had Arabs in the south. There was no notable Arab presence in the Palestinian area. Egypt was coming to the end of its ancient Coptic heritage, ruled by Greeks and then Romans. North Africa had a variety of peoples, including the remnants of the Phoenicians in Tunisia (the former occupants of ancient Carthage); there were also newcomers in North Africa from the barbarian tribes of the Vandals and Visigoths.

The Middle East was, in the main, politically divided between the Byzantine Greeks and the Persians. The former had their centre in Constantinople and they were Greek Christians under a Roman Emperor. The Byzantine Empire encompassed Greece, Asia Minor (modern Turkey), Syria, Palestine and Egypt. At this stage, the Eastern Empire had not formally broken with Western Christianity, although they did not recognise the Roman Christian leader, the Pope, as Head of the Christian Church.[2]

The Persians were led by the Sassanid emperors from 224 to 651 CE. They were the successors to the Parthians (exactly how this was achieved is shrouded in mystery) and they were the last empire in Persia before Islam took over. They ruled from Iraq, but their empire stretched from the west of Iran to the eastern border in Mesopotamia and to the Armenian mountains in the north. Persia, in the early centuries CE, had spread to the frontiers of Syria in the west, to the frontiers of Kush in the east, to the deserts of Arabia in the south, to the mountains of Armenia in the north. It had been liberated in 224 CE by Ardashir, descendant of the legendary Sasan Kings and said

---

2. In the division of Western and Eastern Christians, it should not be overlooked that a major component of Christianity in the early centuries was Coptic Christianity. This was the Christian form adopted in Egypt, the Sudan and Libya. Alexandria was one of the four centres of Christianity, second only to Rome. In 451 CE a church council at Chalcedon in Asia Minor decided that there were two natures in Jesus—a human nature and a divine nature. Many, including the Copts, had argued that there was only a single nature. This brought about a schism between the Coptic Church and the Eastern and Western churches.

to have been surrounded by a supernatural aura known as *farr*, who continued in the line of Sasan, and so the dynasty had been known as the Sassanids.

Moving into the Time of Muhammad

In the time ascribed to the story of Muhammad, the two world powers, Byzantine Greeks and Persian Sassanids, were locked in a political struggle that lasted from 602 to 628 CE. The first round of the battle was won by the Sassanids, the second round by the Byzantine Christians. However, both powers had been weakened by the struggle in terms of their economy and population.

By the time we reach the seventh and eighth centuries CE, the time of Muhammad and the earliest forms of what would eventually become a unified Islam, we find that the Arabs were restricted to the Arabian Peninsula and the southern section of Syria. After that time, there began large movements of Arab peoples, culture and language from their settlements into the known world. They were motivated by conquest of land and by the possibilities of trade.

The development of Arab culture has always been an interesting study. The languages that make up 'Arabic' come from the same Semitic stem, which had originated in the Arabian Peninsula, but great varieties of dialects were known among the tribes. The Arab culture maintained commonalities in the arts and architecture, in social behaviour, in codes of conduct regarding hospitality and family, food and clothing.

It is within this time of political expansion and cultural development in the Middle East that Islam came into being in the form said to have been promoted by the prophet, Muhammad. We turn now to the reasons for this and Islam's central message, as conveyed by its sacred stories.

Notes

There are many general books on Islam. See our previous book:

Lovat, T & Crotty, R (2015). *Reconciling Islam, Christianity and Judaism: Islam's special role in restoring Convivencia.* Heidelberg, Germany: Springer.

For other specialist studies see:

al-Tabari, M (various editors and translators, 1990). *The history of al-Tabari (The history of the prophets & kings – 40 volumes).* New York: SUNY Press.

Lovat, T & Samarayi, I (2009). *The lost story of Islam: Recovery through theology, history and art.* Cologne: Lambert.

Retsö, J (2003). *The Arabs in antiquity: Their history from the Assyrians to the Umayyads.* London: Routledge.

Shatzmiller, M. & Hoyland, R. (2001). *Arabia and the Arabs: From the Bronze Age to the coming of Islam.* London: Routledge.

More general introductions to Islam would include:

Arkoun, M (1994). *Rethinking Islam: Common questions, uncommon answers, today.* Boulder, CA: Westview Press.

Arkoun, M (2002). *The unthought in contemporary Islamic thought.* London: Saqi Books.

Arkoun, M (2006). *Islam: To reform or to subvert.* London: Saqi Books.

Armstrong, K (1992). *Muhammad: A biography of the Prophet.* San Francisco: Harper.

Armstrong, K (2000). *A history of God.* London: Vintage.

Bennett, C (1998). *In search of Muhammad.* London: Continuum International Publishing Group.

Brockopp, J (Ed). (2010). *The Cambridge companion to Muhammad.* London: Cambridge University Press.

Esposito, J (2011). *What everyone needs to know about Islam* (second ed.). Oxford: Oxford University Press.

Lewis, B (2002). *The Arabs in history.* Oxford: Oxford University Press.

Nigosian, SA (2004). *Islam: Its history, teaching, and practices.* Indiana: Indiana University Press.

Ozalp, M (2004). *101 questions you asked about Islam.* Sydney: Brandl and Schlesinger.

Watt WM (1974). *Muhammad: Prophet and statesman.* Oxford: Oxford University Press.

Watt, WM (1953). *Muhammad at Mecca.* Oxford: Clarendon Press.

3
The Message of Islam

Into a world dominated by Byzantine Christians and Sassanid Persians, with Jewish communities dispersed among them, Islam came into existence. Its founder, according to all sources, was the character named Muhammad. Muhammad's teaching was that the true and only God, Allah, had revealed himself in ancient times to Ibrahim. Allah had also revealed himself to a number of prophets, beginning with Adam. These included Issa (known as 'Jesus' in Christianity). Issa was considered to have been the greatest of all the prophets prior to Muhammad himself.

'There is no God but Allah, and Muhammad is his Prophet'. This became the basic statement of the Message of Islam, but there are more components as well.

The Centrepiece of Islam

Allah, the one God, had revealed himself to Ibrahim, the Friend of God.

A central contention of Islam is that both Judaism and Christianity, earlier authentic religions, had strayed far from the Law of God which had first been revealed to Ibrahim. Prior to Muhammad, the prophets (part of both the Jewish and Christian traditions) and, finally, Issa (revered by Christians as Jesus, but said by early Muslims to have been blasphemously misconstrued by them as the Son of God), had been sent by Allah to restore the original faith of Ibrahim. They were however not successful, ultimately because the prophets' traditions, Judaism and Christianity, had failed to heed their message.

The final and last of the prophets was Muhammad. He was directed by Allah to teach the true way to find Allah and peace. Allah revealed to him the beliefs and practices of Islam in a book called the Qur'an or 'The Recitation'. This supplanted both the Hebrew Scriptures and the Christian Gospels. Islam therefore came to see itself as a correction of the Abrahamic tradition and hence the fulfilment of both Judaism's and Christianity's original intentions. Islam knew these two earlier religions as 'Peoples of the Book' because they followed their Scriptures, faulty as they might be.

Islam could be considered the third 'People of the Book' but, in its case, the Book is the Qur'an, the faultless revelation of God and not to be compared to the two earlier collections.

There is an interesting quote in the sacred Qur'an:

> O Peoples of the Book! Why do you dispute about Ibrahim, when the Torah [of Judaism] and the Gospel [of Christianity] were not revealed until after him; do you not then understand? Behold! You are they who disputed about that of which you had knowledge; why then do you dispute about that of which you have no knowledge? And Allah knows while you do not know. Ibrahim was not a Jew or a Christian but he was an upright man, a Muslim, and he was not one of the idolators. Most surely the nearest of people to Ibrahim are those who followed him and this Prophet (Muhammad) and those who believe (Muslims) and Allah is the guardian of the believers.

Surah[1] 3:65-68

---

1. 'Surah' is the Arabic word for chapter and the Qur'an is divided into 114 surahs.

Unpicking the 'Books'

What was the sacred writing, the sacred Qur'an? It was for Muslims the final sacred writing, one that could never be questioned.

However, non-Muslim scholars have found the question of the transmission of the Qur'an fascinating and have attempted to explain it. It must be said that they have also, over the last two centuries, attempted to explain the sacred writings of Judaism, the Hebrew Scriptures, and Christianity, particularly the gospels. By the time ascribed to Muhammad, these had already been gathered into canonical collections. The Hebrew Scriptures were written in Hebrew and Aramaic and there was also a Greek translation. The Christian Scriptures were written in Greek.

We will examine the two earlier collections of Judaism and Christianity first.

Both collections circulated widely in the East and in the Roman world. Roman culture, both East and West, came to be defined, from the fourth century CE, by Christian belief and practice based on these writings. To give some idea of the extent of the two collections of Hebrew and Christian Scriptures, here are summaries of their contents.

The collection of Hebrew Scriptures contains, in its present layout, three major sections.

1. The first section is usually called the *Torah* (its Hebrew title, usually translated as 'Law') or the Pentateuch (which means 'five scrolls' or a 'five-part book' in Greek). These five books are: Genesis, Exodus, Leviticus, Numbers and Deuteronomy.
2. The second section of the Hebrew Scriptures, the *Nevi'im* or Prophets, include the following books: Joshua, Judges, 1 and 2 Samuel, 1 and 2 Kings, Isaiah, Jeremiah, Ezekiel and The Twelve Prophets. Not all of these would make up what we commonly understand as 'prophetic' books.
3. The third section of the Hebrew Scriptures, the *Kethuvim* or Writings, include the following books: Psalms, Proverbs, Job, Song of Solomon, Ruth, Lamentations, Ecclesiastes, Esther, Daniel, Ezra-Nehemiah and 1 and 2 Chronicles.

The Christian Scriptures contain, first of all, the four gospels of Matthew, Mark, Luke and John. Then, there is the Acts of the Apostles, presented as a second volume to the gospel of Luke; fourteen letters of Paul, although there was always doubt about his authorship of at least one of them (the Letter to the Hebrews), and today there is general agreement that some others are not by his hand; the Catholic letters, so-called because they were presumed to be not addressed to particular communities but to the universal (*catholica*) church (although that claim is contentious). The Catholic letters are as follows: the letter of James, two letters of Peter, three letters of John, one letter of Jude; finally, there is the book of Revelation.

Of the Christian Scriptures, the Qur'an has some parallels with the stories that belonged to the four gospels and sometimes has details quite different from those in their canonical forms. There are also some traditions in the Qur'an that are closer to the Apocrypha (see below) than to the canonical writings. It never mentions the other books of the Christian Scriptures, such as those of Paul, the Catholic Letters or the Book of Revelation.

Scholars have become aware of other significant writings that circulated in the early period which were not included in the canonical writings in the fourth century CE. In particular, there were Gnostic texts, usually dated to at least the second century CE, which included the Gospel of Thomas, the Gospel of Philip, the Gospel of Truth and other discourses and religious texts. Also, some Infancy Gospels of Jesus have survived. The copies we have are later but they could reflect earlier traditions. Usually, these texts are in general called The Apocrypha. It is possible that the Qur'an shares some of the traditions from these circles. This is made more plausible by the fact that some of these so-called apocryphal writings were retained by Arabic Christians (some of whom were likely to have been among the first Muslims) after they were banned from mainstream Christianity in the fourth century CE.

Likewise, the stories of Adam, Noah, Ibrahim, Musa (Moses) and David in the Qur'an were different from those in the Jewish Hebrew version. For Muslims, the Qur'anic version is the true one; both the Hebrew Scriptures and the Christian Scriptures were considered deficient and faulty. They had been superseded by the Qur'an.

We are never actually told that Muhammad had contact with the written manuscripts of either Judaism or Christianity. His knowledge, it is usually claimed, would have derived from stories and sayings that came by word of mouth (from Christians, from Jews) in the Arab society in which he lived. There is also a widespread story that, in his days as a trader, he had come into contact with Syrian Christians and had heard their Christian and possibly Jewish stories.

More likely is the following scenario. From the amorphous tradition of narratives about and sayings of Jesus (sometimes simply called the Jesus-Tradition), the gospels had been formed sometime in the second century CE (in their present format). It is possible that early Arab religious tradition had access to a form of the Jesus-Tradition, prior to the concretisation of the gospels in the canonical texts and some of the apocryphal writings.

Despite this difference in textual traditions, the outlines of the essential teachings of Islam are similar to those that would have been circulating in the Jewish and Christian religious settings of the seventh and eighth centuries CE:

- Allah (or God) is the creator of all things and their sustainer;
- He has revealed a sacred law, the *shari'ah* or Pathway[2]; the *shari'ah* contains everything necessary for salvation.
- There are angels, divine beings used by Allah as messengers, as well as good and bad spirits called *djinn*. Evil *djinn* are part of the army of *Iblis* (himself an evil djinn or angel) or *Shaitan* (known as 'Satan' in Judaism and Christianity) who revolted against Allah at the beginning of time;
- There are books of revelation which Allah has, at various times, dictated. The Hebrew Scriptures were given to the Jews and the Gospels to Christians. However, these collections have over time become distorted and their message garbled. The Qur'an is the final book of Allah's revelation. It was dictated to Muhammad and replaces all other books of revelation;
- Allah has chosen prophets and messengers to humankind to teach them the righteous way. The last and greatest of these was Muhammad;
- Allah will be the final judge of humankind; he will reward the righteous in Paradise and punish the wicked in Hell after the resurrection of the dead. Hell is not permanent; eventually humans consigned to Hell will be released.

The message of Islam is not the teaching of Muhammad in the sense that the message of Christianity is the teaching of Jesus. Allah has

---

2. Shari'ah is the Arabic term. It is commonly called 'sharia' in English.

used Muhammad as his spokesperson whereas Jesus is regarded by Christians as a divine being, the author of Christian faith and practice. Likewise, the notion of ethics in Islam is different from that in Christianity or Judaism. For the Muslim, there is the *shari'ah*, the one guiding rule of life that covers all aspects of living, secular and religious. Christian ethics are based on the Christian Scriptures but have been developed further over time.

A useful way to consider the difference between Jesus and the Bible for Christians and Muhammad and the Qur'an for Muslims is the following oft-written phrase:

> In Christianity, the Word became Flesh; in Islam, the Word became Book.

Notes

For further reading see:

> Leaman, O (ed), (2006). *The Qur'an: An encyclopaedia*. London: Routledge.
> Qutb, S (2009). *In the shade of the Qur'an* (vols. 1-13). London: Islamic Foundation.
> Sardar, Z (2006). *What do Muslims believe?* London: Granta.
> Warraq, I (1998). *The origins of the Qur'an*. New York: Prometheus Books.

4
The Beginnings of Islam and the Prophet, Muhammad

It was amongst the Arabs, as described above, in the vast expanses of the Arabian Peninsula, that Islam first emerged. As we have seen, these Arab people had achieved a high degree of culture and were adept in agriculture and trade. Islam was an Arab religious venture and we need to understand what we can of its origins.

To do this, we must have some knowledge of Islam's founder, the character who became known as 'Muhammad'. That is no easy task. Who was the historical Muhammad? We also need to see in more detail that Muhammad's role in Islam is not the same as the role of Jesus in mainstream Christianity.

Further, we need to see that a search for an historical Muhammad differs from the more recent search for an historical Jesus—something that Christian scholars often overlook.

The Beginnings of Islam

We have already mentioned that a series of Arab states had been established in the centuries before the time of Islam. In the south of the Arabian Peninsula, they were each ruled by a leader who was both a political leader and a religious high-priest. The religion of these people included polytheism, the worship of many gods. There were three particular gods well known among the tribes: a Moon god, a Sun goddess and another god who was probably represented by the Evening star, Venus. Religious ritual consisted of sacrifices offered at due times, and pilgrimages to the respective holy places. The tribes had priests who performed their duties under the surveillance of the king-priest.

In the north of the Arabian Peninsula, however, a more ancient way of life had been preserved, although by the seventh century CE, it was beginning to disintegrate. This ancient way of life had been based on tribes rather than political states, as in the south. Stability was maintained not by a king-priest but by tribal solidarity, by which the members of the tribe were assured that they could rely on fellow tribal members for protection and sustenance.

This loyalty to one another in the tribe was the essential quality of the tribal life. It was known as *muruwwa*, or literally something like 'manliness'. The key ideas contained in the word were 'bravery, patience, protection of the weak', and the Arabs associated with this term another word: *hamasa* or 'fortitude'. Because tribal life was arduous and demanding, survival depended on fortitude, each member had to play their part to the full in tribal life. If it should have happened that the rights of one member were trampled on, then the tribe took common vengeance. *Muruwwa* demanded this, and the action was accompanied by *hamasa*.

Tribal honour understood in this way was, therefore, the basis of any ethical system in the tribes. Right and wrong could be distinguished. Arab tribal poets sang of the mighty deeds of their past and those deeds became exemplars for subsequent generations. The poets also sang of the evil deeds performed by other tribes. Listening to these songs from childhood, the Arab in the north would have been trained to distinguish a good life from an evil life.

Among the northern tribes, there were also many gods. However, there had been, around the seventh century CE, a new development.

Some religious preachers proclaimed that the most important god, perhaps the only god, was *al 'ilah* or 'The God'. The term *al 'ilah* has later been elided as 'Allah'. Allah, his proponents taught, lived in the sky but he provided rain and crop fertility for those who believed in him. He was a High God, creator of all and sustainer of the cosmic order. However, the worship of Allah was not the common form of religious adherence at that time. Most Arabs had access to many gods.

There were places for the worship of gods in the north: simple rock formations or a tree, surrounded by a sacred enclosure. Tribal people would meet on occasion at these sacred places and share a meal of a sacrificed animal. At certain times of the year, there were pilgrimages to these same places. However, there was no priesthood —unlike among the more sophisticated Arabs in the south. By the end of the fifth century CE, one of the Arab tribes, the Quraysh already described above, had seized the area around the city of Mecca. As we have seen, they made it their religious centre and they honoured its shrine, called the Ka'aba or 'Cube', built over a large black stone, probably of meteoric origin. The shrine also honoured a number of the tribal gods, tradition (Islamic, and perhaps biased) mentioning three hundred idols within the Ka'aba.

It was in the seventh century CE that this northern tribal structure began to break up and Mecca was a prime example. Why did the tribal structure in Mecca falter? The political states in the south wanted to trade with the areas around the Mediterranean. A major trade route went through Mecca and it began to enjoy prosperity never before known. Arab merchants in Mecca began to forget their tribal roots. They felt that they must look after their own interests and the greatest value was no longer *muruwwa,* but increased wealth.

Mecca was still governed in name by the tribal leaders and there were the rudimentary institutions of Bedouin governance with significant decisions being made by a council of elders representing the tribes. There was also however a growing tension between the wealthy traders and those who had to find a living as farmers and workers for the trade market. New wealth had established a new social system and the tribal life was haemorrhaging.

This would be the Arab context from which Islam sprang. It was a complex situation from an historical, geographical, economic and cultural viewpoint. More importantly, it represented a religious turning point. Central to that religious turning-point is in the story of the character, Muhammad, and the revelation from Allah that is claimed in his story.

The Prophet, Muhammad

In order to construct a methodology for understanding the events of Muhammad's life, we should first compare this search for an historical Muhammad to the search for an historical Jesus amongst recent Christian academics. Indeed, studies of the historical Muhammad have been influenced by this earlier search.

The First Search for the Historical Jesus took place during the nineteenth century. The Western world of the previous century had been shaken to its roots by the contention that science and history, not religion and tradition, were the valid sources of knowledge. As a result, scholarship of the time was characterised by a concerted effort to examine all areas of learning and to eliminate the scourge of superstition. This scholarly effort would naturally have a particularly sharp edge when it came to areas of religious learning and its purported claims.

In this context, it is understandable that scientific methodology would be applied to the Bible in order to find out what was worthwhile and what should be discarded. After all, the Bible was already regarded as a source for ancient history and also of contemporary Jewish and Christian devotion. The only historical knowledge about Babylonia and Assyria, for instance, came from the Bible. However, the two areas of history and piety did not sit well together. Scholars re-read the Bible, incorporating the Hebrew Scriptures and the Christian Scriptures, as if it were one more historical text. Obviously, if Christianity was to be accepted as a believable way of life, a major project would have to be the reconstruction of an historical life of Jesus.

What were the historical sources on which such a life of Jesus could be based? There were four versions of his life in the four canonical gospels of Matthew, Mark, Luke and John. These gospels were analysed, and discrepancies were found in events, in sayings and in chronology. It was decided that the original sources were Mark and a hypothetical Sayings Gospel, known by scholars as Q. Matthew and Luke were said to have been constructed on the basis of these two sources.[3] John depended on other sources.

By the early twentieth century, many Christian scholars had concluded that it might never be possible to recover an historical Jesus (see Chilton & Evans, 1994; Bultmann, 1958).

Up to the 1950s, while most Christians presumably still accepted the gospels as more or less factual eye-witness accounts, there were many Christian academics who doubted that anything could be known about the historical Jesus apart from the fact that he probably existed. On the basis of his life and sayings, later Christians had constructed a 'Jesus' on which Christianity was based. In other words, the person known as 'Jesus' by Christians was not entirely fictional but, even if he was, it would not undermine the essence of Christian belief.

They consoled themselves by rejecting any need for an historical Jesus, distinguishing between the Jesus of History, the figure that might be reconstructed by the objective historian, and the Christ of Faith, the figure preached and proclaimed by believing Christians. All that Christian faith required, they explained to each other, was the message of Jesus as told in the gospel story. Whether an historical Jesus ever existed, or whether he factually delivered the message attributed to him, came to be seen as immaterial to many scholars (see particularly Bultmann, 1958).

By the mid-1950s, however, other scholars began to murmur discontentedly with the results of the First Search. They found the sharp division between the Jesus of History and the Christ of Faith to be disconcerting. They began a Second Search (although at the time it was called the '*New* Search'). The movement began with a lecture by the great German scholar, Ernst Käsemann in 1953. His ideas were taken up by other scholars (Bornkamm, 1956; Robinson, 1959). These Second Searchers were certain that they were more in control of the gospel texts as literature and that much had been learned in the preceding fifty years about the background history and culture of the times in which Jesus had lived, particularly from Flavius Josephus, the Jewish historian who minutely described those times.

---

3. At the present moment, most scholars would still agree that some form of Mark, not necessarily the canonical form established in the fourth century CE, was an original source but many doubt if there ever was a Sayings Gospel Q.

They felt they could present a more fleshed-out Life of Jesus. While they could not expand much on his birth story, they could identify that a turning point had occurred in his life when he met with John the Baptist and was baptised by him. This would have led to his ministry in Galilee, his subsequent journey to the capital city of Jerusalem and his execution by crucifixion under Pontius Pilate. An historical Jesus could be identified behind these pivotal actions as a teacher, an exorcist and a healer who ministered primarily to the poor and marginalised. His divinity, his resurrection and his ascension were left in abeyance (Robinson, 1959).

The Second Search was a great relief to many practising Christian scholars. There was sufficient historical underpinning in its findings on which to base the major claims of Christianity. At least Jesus had lived, preached, died on the cross and was resurrected (in some way).

The Second Search was however to be quickly overtaken by new discoveries. The Dead Sea Scrolls were gradually discovered from 1947 (Martinez & Tigchelaar, 1997-8; Vanderkam, rev. ed. 2010; Golb, 1995). They seemed to talk of a sect that was somewhat similar to the Christians and very much like the Essenes, a Jewish monastic sect once described by the historian Josephus. Perhaps Jesus had belonged to the Essene sect; perhaps his followers had come from the sect; almost certainly, the scrolls were seen to be describing the background of early Christianity. There was a further question: was there ever really a Christianity founded around an historical character, Jesus, or was Christianity really a construction after the event, the work of a myth rather than in any way historically grounded?

There had also been another discovery in Egypt in 1945 of papyrus texts written in Coptic (late Egyptian), although it was not until the 1960s that the texts became available (Robinson, 1990). They were Gnostic texts, previously unknown (see mention of the Apocrypha in chapter 3). The Gnostics had been regarded as Christian heretics.

As mentioned earlier, amongst the texts were the Gospel of Thomas, the Gospel of Philip and the Gospel of Truth. Some of the sayings in these gospels were very similar to those in the Christian gospels. Which had come first: the Gnostic gospels or the 'Christian' gospels?

All of this new thinking gave rise to a Third Search for the Historical Jesus. The Third Searchers made use of the new advances:

literary analysis of first century CE texts (which included not only the Christian canonical literature but the Dead Sea Scrolls and hypothetical antecedents of some Gnostic texts), historical enquiry into the late Second Temple period in Palestine together with the application of models and perspectives from a number of disciplines such as cultural anthropology, social history, sociology and feminist studies.

There were many attempts, using these methods, to define and ground the 'Historical Jesus'. The answers were varied: he was an eschatological prophet, a Hellenistic Cynic teacher, a subversive wisdom teacher, a social prophet, an eschatological prophet of the present and coming Kingdom, a Mediterranean Jewish peasant, an egalitarian prophet of Wisdom, the 'Wicked Priest' spoken of in the Dead Sea Scrolls (see Crotty, 1996).

There was an immediate problem for the Third Searchers. They produced too many competing Jesus-es. They could not all be right. For instance, he could not be both an illiterate peasant and a literary purveyor of holy Wisdom sayings. Furthermore, many Third Searchers required that any Christian teaching should be based on the Historical Jesus that they might favour. The arguments over the Third Search still continue and no one answer is accepted by a majority.

Applying the historical method to Muhammad

Our intention is to go no further in this Christian endeavour.

Instead, we must look at the comparable problem in Islam. Who was the historical Muhammad (Peters 1991; Zeitlin, 2007)? At first sight, he would seem to be a more apposite subject for historical enquiry by academics. He was strenuously said by his tradition to be human and not divine; in spite of typical legendary birth stories, he is nonetheless, unlike Jesus, acknowledged by his tradition to have been a man born in the normal way with two parents; he lived in the Arabian Peninsula and married and had children. From the stories, it appears we can calculate real dates, including dates for his conversion and mission; his death was similar to that of most humans (although it is believed he was taken straight into heaven) and his career was reported by reputable authorities, even if the reporting came much later.

Nonetheless, there are still problems with writing a life of Muhammad. We are fairly well informed by reputable history, including that of the Romans, about life in first century Palestine and in particular about Jewish Jerusalem. Hence, we can understand the context for a life of Jesus. On the other hand, there is no historian the equivalent of Flavius Josephus and no texts like the Dead Sea Scrolls or the Gnostic texts to provide the same sort of contextual and intellectual insight into early Islam, as we have into early Christianity. If all that Christian scholars knew about Christian origins was background material recorded in some Egyptian or Syrian sources from a later date, then they would be in much the same position as the Islamic historian.

In fact, by comparison, little is known about Mecca at the time of Muhammad, its political and economic connections or its religious culture. Scholars today debate about the situation in the Arabian Peninsula at that time, and there is actually no physical evidence left of the *Ummahs* (the Islamic communities) said to have been established in Medina and Mecca under Muhammad.

Another problem is that the Christian gospels described the factual events in which Jesus was involved and also some of his sayings. We can certainly grant that scholars have remained divided as to which of these actions were actually historical and which sayings were Jesus' own words. On the other hand, the Qur'an does not relay the life of Muhammad at all. The Qur'an consists of a discourse, a monologue from Allah via the angel Jibril (known as Gabriel in Jewish and Christian texts). It is text without any real historical context. It relays the words of Allah without context or chronology.

In Christian theology, it is the events of the life of Jesus—his baptism, his death, his resurrection—that bring salvation; in Islam, it is the teaching of the Qur'an that performs this function. Muhammad's life is not vital to the achievement of salvation as Jesus' divine life was essential for Christian salvation. To find out the details of Muhammad's life, the scholar must go to a lesser sacred set of writings concerning Islam's historical tradition.

When however would the final version of the Qur'an have been historically redacted? Was it during the lifetime of the Prophet, as the main Islamic studies maintain? Or was it during the time of the first Caliphs (a 'Deputy' who led Islam after the death of Muhammad) or even much later? Perhaps, it has been stated, Islam as we recognise it was really the work of al-Tabari some 200-300 years on from the supposed events of Medina and Mecca in the 600s CE. As might be expected, scholars, Muslim and non-Muslim, are very much divided in this debate.

In November, 2014, it was announced that the University of Birmingham had discovered, among its resources in storage, parts from an early Qur'an. These have been Carbon-14 dated to only twenty to forty years after the conventional date given for Muhammad's birth. This important fact will have repercussions on the studies of the relationship of the historical Muhammad to the text of the Qur'an. On the surface, it seems to corroborate the popular view that the Qur'an was assembled in the lifetime of Muhammad but not the more scholarly view in Islam that the fully transcribed text of the Qur'an came from a period well after Muhammad's death, during the time of the third successor, the Uthman caliphate. Furthermore, Muslim and non-Muslims scholars are now considering the implications of the fragments being possibly from a time coinciding with Muhammad's infancy or even prior to his birth. At the very least, this is likely to intensify research about the dates ascribed to his birth, matters that are not of themselves especially crucial to the story. Of greater interest is the potential for scholarship that would show that elements of what would eventually form part of the Qur'an could have come from an earlier time altogether, a view consistent with the very complex and multi-layered history that constitutes Islam's origins, as shown above.

Nonetheless, it must be said that, even if the composition of the Qur'an took place in the lifetime of Muhammad, the Muslims who handed it on and noted it down, as they said, on 'scraps of leather, bone and in their hearts' never claimed that these were meant to be the actual words of Muhammad; the claim was always that these were the words of Allah, transmitted through Muhammad. Later tradition stated that the original Qur'an was inscribed on tablets of gold in heaven and recited from these tablets to Muhammad by the Angel, Jibril.

It follows therefore that, between the academic study of Jesus and that of Muhammad, there are at least two significant differences. First, Jesus achieved his ends by deeds, according to the version of

Christianity that became 'orthodox' in the fourth century CE.[4] This orthodox view had it that he was born of a virgin, preached a mission to Jews and Gentiles, then was crucified in a bloody sacrifice for the atonement of human sinfulness, was physically resurrected from the tomb and physically ascended into heaven. For orthodox Christian doctrine, the facts are essential. If Jesus did not die and rise again, then the Christian faith would be considered fraudulent by most believers. That at least has been the traditional position in Christianity.

The same is not true of Islam. Whatever may be said historically about Muhammad, it is the Qur'an that is of the greater religious importance. In this sense, the history of Jesus is considered by Christians as essential to their faith; the history of Muhammad is not, for the Muslim, of quite the same order, albeit he is revered fervently as the greatest of the Prophets. Nonetheless, it is the Qur'an that is essential to Muslim faith.

Second, there are the four versions of the gospel story of Jesus and they were written within a century after the life of Jesus. They contain many facts, albeit there is the problem that they conflict with each other in part. For many Christian believers, these differences must be reconciled since 'infallible gospels' cannot be contrary to each other. In Islam, however, there is only one version of the Qur'an and only a few facts from the life of Muhammad can be elicited from it. Even accepting that it is infallible does not ensure any facts about Muhammad's personal story. The actual accounts of his life would seem to have been written a long time after the central ascribed event of receiving the Qur'anic revelation.

After the death of Muhammad, there is historical silence. Perhaps there are a few references by Christian scholars to him, but this is doubtful. There are actually no references by early Muslims to Muhammad. In the 690s CE, one of the Caliphs inscribed Muhammad's name on a monument. It was not until the 800s CE, however, that biographies came to be written. By then, the character who became known as Muhammad had presumably been dead for

---

4. The version of Jesus events and their chronology used in the Searches has been taken largely from Roman Christianity. This became almost the sole representative of Christianity from the time of Constantine in the fourth century CE. Mark, Matthew and Luke were Roman Christian gospels. John was edited and adapted by Roman Christians.

two centuries or more. Moreover, whatever biographies came to pass did not agree with each other in their details. The question for scholarship, if not for every believer, is then whether we are looking here at a constructed religious history rather than a history of facts, in our modern sense of history.

Some of the early traditions about Muhammad do give us information about his life. The *Sirat Rasul Allah* (the Life of the Apostle of Allah) is taken to be the standard life of Muhammad. It was originally composed by Ibn Ishaq who died in 767 CE. It gave a richly detailed life of Muhammad with the integration of some Qur'anic materials. His work no longer exists and the only amended edition that has survived was achieved by his student Ibn Hisham who died in 833CE. Ibn Hisham explained his redaction method:

> ...I confine myself to the Prophet's biography and omit some of the things which Ibn Ishaq has recorded in his book in which there is no mention of the Apostle and about which the Qur'an says nothing and which are not relevant to anything in this book or an explanation of it; poems which he quotes that no authority of poetry whom I have met knows of; things which it is disgraceful to discuss; matters which would distress certain people; and such reports as al-Bakka'i told me he could not accept as trustworthy—all these things I have omitted. (*The Life of Muhammad: A translation of Ishaq's Sirat Rasul Allah*, Oxford 1955, p.691)

In other words, what is recorded about the life of Muhammad by Ibn Ishaq is couched in terms of caution.

What follows is an outline of the history of Muhammad, using the sources above, as it would be acceptable to believing Muslims. Once more, it must be made clear that doubts about events in his life have no effect on the essentials of Islam, albeit they will be of enduring importance to the piety of many Muslims.

Somewhere around 570 CE, so it is believed, Muhammad was born into the Quraysh tribe. He was born in Mecca but orphaned in early life. After that, he was brought up by his grandfather and then an uncle. Little is known about his early life apart from some later traditions which are not reliable. However, they do recount that he had travelled as a child to Syria with a trading caravan and a Christian monk, called Bahira, had welcomed the boy as a great prophet. This is similar to the earlier Christian tradition of Jesus being acknowledged in the Temple of Jerusalem by Simeon and so scholarship naturally suspects it is part of a borrowed tradition rather than necessarily factual.

Muhammad was employed by a widow named Khadija, who was engaged in commerce in Mecca. Muhammad worked in the business and eventually married her. Together, they had a number of children, including Fatima, a daughter who would go on to become part of the legend behind the Shia sect of Islam. No more is known of this period in his life.

Around the age of forty, it is said, the life of Muhammad underwent a dramatic change. Muslim tradition tells us that he was dissatisfied with the religious life found in Mecca, finding it worldly and unjust and riven with the worship of many gods. He used to go to a cave on a hillside outside the town and spend long hours in meditation. During one of these religious sessions, he was confronted by the 'The God', *al 'ilah* or Allah. Sometimes the confrontation is spoken of as one of direct contact; at other times, Muhammad is said to have spoken to Allah through an intermediary, the Angel Jibril.

Whatever the facts might be, the heart of the story is about the experience he had and how it changed his life completely. He now knew that he was the Prophet of Allah. Muhammad would go on to describe the experience of this meeting with Allah in the following way:

> I swear by the star when it goes down.
> Your companion does not err, nor does he go astray;
> Nor does he speak out of desire.
> It is naught but revelation that is revealed,
> The Lord of Mighty Power has taught him,
> The Lord of Strength; so he attained completion,
> And he is in the highest part of the horizon.
> Then he drew near, then he bowed down.
> So he was the measure of two bows or closer still.
> And He revealed to His servant what He revealed.

Surah 53: 10

He also described himself being designated to write down his experiences in the Qur'an:

> Recite in the name of your Lord Who created.
> He created man from a clot [of blood].
> Recite and your Lord is Most Honorable,
> Who taught [to write] with the pen
> Taught man what he knew not.
>
> *Surah* 96:1-5

After this call from Allah, Muhammad became a religious preacher, in the way of the ancient prophets. He was certain that he was not handing on his own ideas, but those of Allah. The divine call had impelled him to speak out and he became a *rasul*, literally one who is sent by God to proclaim a message; Muhammad was considered to be a *rasul* to all humanity. He must preach.

According to the story, Muhammad felt himself directed towards a new way of life with new ideals. At first, his preaching in Mecca attracted only friends and relatives. Many despised his preaching and he was ridiculed by the Meccans generally. According to the story, even his own Arab clan within the Quraysh tribe was unsympathetic.

This is understandable. Muhammad is said to have rejected the many gods of Mecca, highly valued by the townspeople. He preached the oneness of Allah. He also demanded social justice and threatened dire punishment on those who refused to follow his directives. For the powerful, including the traders, in Mecca, this seemed a direct threat, in much the same way that the Magna Carta was seen as a threat to kings and much of the establishment in England in the thirteenth century. After all, the establishment in Mecca similarly had vested interests in its commercial life staying as it was, and they did not want anyone interfering with the social structure that saw them enjoying powerful positions in their society.

Hence, the story tells of Muhammad facing constant rebuff. He moved to Ta'if, about 80 kilometres from Mecca, but the venture did not produce any better results. Then, his wife Khadija died and, as she had been his chief support, this was yet another setback. Nonetheless, there was finally to be a change in fortune.

Twelve years after the first revelation to Muhammad, an Arab group of six men came on pilgrimage to Mecca from the northern city of Yathrib; this was said to be in about 622 CE. It was a turning-point. By chance, as the story goes, they heard Muhammad preach his message about the Oneness of Allah and the need for social justice among the people. They were impressed by his preaching, a receptivity not accorded him by the Meccans. The group returned to Yathrib and spread the word of Muhammad the *rasul* among their fellow citizens.

Yathrib had its own problems. There were about 3000 inhabitants and they were divided into two Arab tribes, hostile to each other, and a group of Arab Jews who lived on the fringes of this divided society. No central authority had been able to unite the three sectors, and order was only maintained by the fear of public violence and bloodshed.

The group that had visited Mecca persuaded their fellow citizens to invite Muhammad to come to Yathrib and become its religious and political leader. They wanted him to preach his new message and to heal the wounds of enmity. Thereby, they hoped that they could form a community from the different groups. In fact, Muhammad was a prophet in need of a place of safety; Yathrib was a city in need of a prophet. They matched each other well.

Muhammad agreed. His journey from Mecca to Yathrib became known among Muslims as the *Hijra* or 'Emigration'. This journey has been taken to mark the real beginning of Islam as a religion. By leaving Mecca with a small group of followers, Muhammad broke with the old tribal organisation, whether in the north or south, and established a religion with its own institutions. This new organisation would take the form of a religious society known as the *Ummah* or 'community'.

The idea of an *Ummah* came from the tribal experience. However, it was wider and not constrained by blood relationship or common history. From then until today, all professing Muslims are members of what is referred to as the *Ummah Wahida*, literally the 'one', or universal, Community (of Allah); in other words, these are God's People. Yathrib laid the groundwork for the *Ummah*: the old solidarity of separate tribal groups was replaced by a system of social cohesion; the former allegiances to tribal gods were replaced by the worship of the One God, Allah. Any subsequent Islamic community would become part of the universal *Ummah*. The *Ummah* was deemed to be shaped by the *shari'ah*, the law (or belief and practice) of Islam.

The momentous nature of the establishment of Islam in Yathrib must be appreciated. For Muslims of all times, this was the beginning of a new era. It should have taken place in the past, including being established in Judaism and Christianity by the earlier prophets. Instead, it had taken a Muhammad to put things aright. Thus, the time of the beginning of Islam was distinguished from *Jahiliyyah*, the Age of Ignorance. *Jahiliyyah* represented the earlier time of social divisions, of religious fragmentation, of lawlessness and of sexual impropriety. It had engulfed not only Arabs, but the entire world, including ultimately Judaism and Christianity, both made for better things. This was what life was like pre-Islam. With the advent of Islam, a new era had begun.

From this time, Yathrib became known as *Medinat annabi* or 'City of the Prophet'. This was eventually shortened to Medina. The word *medina* actually means a 'legal district' in Aramaic, and the term had been borrowed by the Arabs.

Medina, where the community of Islam was first organised, and Mecca, the birthplace of Muhammad and the home to the Ka'aba built by Ibrahim, have become the sacred cities of Islam. Mecca rates first and Medina second. A third sacred city is Jerusalem, where tradition describes a mystical journey of Muhammad to address all the previous prophets:

> Glory be to Him Who made His servant to go on a night from the Sacred Mosque [in Mecca] to the Further Mosque [in Jerusalem] of which We have blessed the precincts, so that We may show to him some of Our signs.
>
> Surah 17:1

A later expansion on the tradition claimed that, while in Jerusalem, Muhammad ascended into heaven on a horse and came before the throne of Allah. He then returned. The present Mosque of Omar in Jerusalem, first built in the late seventh century CE, purports to mark the precise place of this ascension from a raised rock. It is known as 'the Dome of the Rock', the most sacred site in Jerusalem for Muslims, and a place that has been at the centre of much twentieth and twenty-first century politics around Jerusalem, a sacred city to

Jews, Christians and Muslims for different and sometimes opposing reasons.

The *Ummah* of Islam in Medina, it is said, immediately recognised certain categories of Muslims in its community. There were the Companions or *sahavah*, the privileged early associates of Muhammad; these had been his followers from the time of his first call by Allah. Then, there were the Exiles who had shared his emigration to Medina. Finally, there were the Helpers, the people of Medina and its surrounds who had joined him after his arrival in Medina.

Although Muhammad had been welcomed into Medina, there were still problems. First of all, Medina had economic difficulties and there were threats from Mecca because of this. It had been customary among Arabs for raids to be mounted on caravans for booty. Weaker opposition might simply hand over the booty; on occasion, the encounters were bloody. Pressed by need, the Muslims of Medina engaged in this activity. Some less powerful groups in the area saw what was happening and asked to be protected. In so doing, so it is said, they implicitly accepted the leadership of Muhammad and their consequent conversion to Islam. The Muslims in Medina were spreading outwards.

The mechanism for this outreach was called *jihad* or 'striving'. As part of this striving, the name became associated with the 'holy wars' that were inevitably waged as the Muslim believers moved steadily into new sites. There was nothing particularly unusual for such wars to be waged at that time, and it does not necessitate Islam being cast as an unusually hostile or violent religion, as is often done in Western commentary. Like most religions, Islam developed first in a particular culture and took on many of the ways of its surroundings. What Islam added to the prevalent war-waging of its times was a particularly sharp religious interpretation.

According to Muslim belief, Allah ensured victory in such a holy war and the whole enterprise was not merely seen as a political move dictated by economic necessity, but rather as a religious ritual. Because Muslims were following the true God whose purpose was to form a people in his own name, then this God would guarantee their victory. It is not altogether a different theme from one found commonly in the Hebrew and Christian Scriptures. So, *Jihad* does not primarily connote the imposition of Islam by force, although that may have certainly been the effect at times and, as suggested, the understanding of later times.

Political adhesion to the Muslims necessarily brought in its train religious change. Those who sought the security of Muhammad's protection needed to accept Muhammad's religious system as well. While the Arab tribes had little choice, Jews and Christians in the area of the Arabian Peninsula could become a part of the *Ummah* by accepting the status of a protected minority that did not have to give up their own religions. Thus, the idea of the Peoples of the Book, already mentioned, protected these religious minorities. Those who adhered to the Hebrew Scriptures or the Gospels, faulty as they might be in the Muslim mind, were given the privilege of retaining their own religion, even if it was regarded as defective.

These protected and, in many cases, well respected minority groups were known as the *dhimmi* ('protected') peoples. The policy of protecting such minorities, particularly Jews and Christians, under Muslim rule has been, in recent times, called *dhimmitude*. We will say more about it later.

In 624 CE, it is said, Muhammad led a war party of three hundred warriors from Medina on a raid against a Meccan caravan at a place called Badr. They were victorious despite the smallness of their number. The rage of the Meccans and of Muhammad's own tribe, the Quraysh, was explosive. Because of the victory, however, more Bedouin followers joined Muhammad.

In the following year, however, Muhammad's still small army of seven hundred Muslims was defeated by the Quyrash (numbering 3000) at a place called Uhud, not far from Medina. This caused some soul searching. If Badr had been a sign of Allah's protection of the *Ummah*, how was defeat at Badr to be interpreted? The answer given by Muhammad emphasised what he saw as the principal element of all Islamic religion—submission. This was at a later date explained in the Qur'an:

> If a wound has afflicted you [at Uhud], a wound like it has also afflicted the [unbelieving] people; and We bring these days to men by turns, and that Allah may know those who believe and take martyrs from among you; and Allah does not love the unjust.

And a soul will not die but with the permission of Allah. The term is fixed; and whoever desires the reward of this world, I shall give him of it, and whoever desires the reward of the hereafter I shall give him of it, and I will reward the faithful. And how many a prophet has fought side by side with many worshippers of the Lord; so they did not become weak-hearted on account of what befell them in Allah's Path, nor did they weaken, nor did they abase themselves; and Allah loves the determined. And their saying was no other than: Our Lord! Forgive us our faults and our extravagance in our affairs and make firm our feet and help us against the unbelieving people.So Allah gave them the reward of this world and the better reward of the hereafter and Allah loves those who do good [to others].

Surah 3: 140-148

What we can see from this development is that an outline of Islam was taking shape and it went like this: there is an order of things in the world determined by Allah, and Muslims must submit themselves to this order absolutely. This is what is meant by following the *shari'ah* or the 'Pathway of Allah', the following of which will lead to salvation.

Medina was, by this point, openly pitted against Mecca. The struggle came to a head when the Quraysh and their supporters attacked Medina. A later tradition tells of 10,000 Meccan troops and some disenchanted Jews being massed against the army of Muhammad. Muhammad made clever use of trenches to disable the Meccan cavalry and won the battle. Consequently, this became known as the Battle of the Ditch. Upon their return, the Medinan army wreaked vengeance on what they saw as a treacherous Jewish population. Some eight hundred of them were executed and the first of many tragic stories of Abrahamic sibling warfare had begun.

Subsequently, Mecca and Medina made a truce that lasted for ten years. During these years of uneasy peace in Medina, Muhammad's time was taken up with the problems of everyday living in the *Ummah*. Moral directives were devised to enable the Muslim people to live out their submission to Allah. Then, in 630 CE, the truce with Mecca came to an end.

The Meccans attacked a Muslim tribe, leading Muhammad to gather his forces and to march on Mecca. The Meccans soon saw that they were surrounded and they surrendered. Mecca fell to Muhammad and the Muslims. At once, he enforced the observance of

Islam on the city. He destroyed the images in the Ka'aba, but retained its structure. After all, it was honoured as a shrine established by Ibrahim to the worship of the One God, later 'desecrated' with god-images by the Quraysh. By this stage, Islam had control of Mecca and Medina and most of the surrounding land.

According to the story, Muhammad returned to Medina and he died there in 632 CE. He left behind an Islam that was on the march, quickly incorporating the other tribes in the Arabian Peninsula into its political and religious structures. Eventually, the spread would reach the borders of the Byzantine Empire. Islam was on the move.

One of the sayings in the Qur'an expresses its sense of self-confidence at this time:

> You are indeed the best community that has ever been produced among humanity. You demand that what is right is done; you forbid what is wrong to be done.

Surah 3

In Conclusion

Is the story of the creation of Islam historically reliable? There are many scholars who would reply in the negative and claim that we know little about an historical Muhammad or the historical founding of Islam. If that is accepted, then the answer is the same as the response to the problems of Christian scholars of early Christian history. The story is the important item and becoming overly concerned about its historicity can actually be a distraction for the believer.

It must be understood however that most Muslim believers would still stand by the historical accuracy of the life of Muhammad and the story of early Islam. In more recent times, Islamic scholars have strongly maintained the historical literalness and accuracy of their stories. This has sometimes caused a gulf in any dialogue with Jews or Christians. Unlike many earlier Muslims who understood well the nature of religious myth and legend, modern Muslim religious education has left many religious believers with an adherence to literalism that is not well supported by the known facts. This is beginning to change in our own times. As Muslim scholars and others witness the sometimes devastating effects of fundamentalism and literalism, never seen more glaringly than in the spectre of the so-called 'Islamic State' (ISIS or ISIL—see ch. 9 below), there is a growing sense that Islam must be rescued from such skewed and badly informed ideologies. Part of the reaction is seen in a more urgent sense of unpicking and ascertaining the reality behind the story of its foundations. What is the essence of Islam that sits behind the alleged facts?

Notes

Translations of the Qur'an throughout this book have been taken from Taqi-ed-Din Al-Hilali M. and Muhsin Khan, M. (translators), *Interpretation of the Meanings of the Noble Quran*, Dar-us-Salam Publications, New York. http://www.dar-us-salam.com

For more technical information on the beginnings of Islam, see:

> Ohlig, KH & Puin, GR (Eds), (2009). *The hidden origins of Islam: New research into its early history.* New York: Prometheus Books.

This chapter has covered a series of areas where serious scholarship has been taking place and still is. The intention was simply to record the more general lines of agreement on the following topics:

First, on the Search for the Historical Jesus, the following contain a variety of approaches:

> Bornkamm, G (1960). *Jesus of Nazareth.* New York: Harper.
> Bultmann, R (1958, trans. 2005). *Myth and Christianity: An inquiry into the possibility of religion without myth.* New York: Noonday Press.
> Chilton, B & Evans, C (Eds), (1994). *Studying the historical Jesus: Evaluations of the current state of research.* Leiden: Brill.
> Crossan, JD (1993). *The historical Jesus: The life of a Mediterranean Jewish peasant.* Melbourne: Collins Dove.
> Crotty, R (1996/1). *The Jesus question: The historical search.* Melbourne: Harper-Collins.

Robinson, J (1959). *New quest for the historical Jesus and other essays.* London: SCM.
Sanders, E (1985). *Jesus and Judaism.* Philadelphia: Fortress.

On the Dead Sea Scrolls, there has been much written of late. First of all, there are several good translations. Two can be recommended for the general reader:

Martinez, FG & Tigchelaan, E (1997-8). *The Dead Sea Scrolls (two volumes).* Leiden: Brill.
Vermes, G (1997). *The complete Dead Sea Scrolls in English* (complete edition). London: Allen Lane Penguin.

There are also some general introductions to Scroll research that fill in much of the background. They differ in their quality, and some should only be used with caution:

Fitzmyer, J (2009). *The impact of the Dead Sea Scrolls.* New York: Paulist Press.
Golb, N (1995). *Who wrote the Dead Sea Scrolls? The search for the secret of Qumran.* London: BCA.
Shanks, H (1992). *Understanding the Dead Sea Scrolls.* New York: Random House.
Vanderkam, J (rev ed 2010). *The Dead Sea Scrolls today.* Grand Rapids: William B Eerdemans.

For a translation of the Gnostic texts, see:

Robinson, J (rec ed 1990). *The Nag Hammadi Library.* San Francisco: HarperCollins.

For an introduction to the Gnostic writings and their thought, a good start can be made with some of the prolific work of Elaine Pagels:
Pagels, E (1979). *The Gnostic Gospels.* London: Weidenfeld and Nicholson.
King, K (2003). *What is Gnosticism?* Cambridge, MN: Harvard University Press.

For readers seeking greater depth on Christian Gnosticism, consult:

Franzmann, M (2001). *Jesus in the Nag Hammadi Writings.* Edinburgh: T& T Clark.

Franzmann, M. (2011). Gnostic portraits of Jesus. In D Burkett (Ed.), *The Blackwell companion to Jesus* (pp. 160-175). London: Blackwell Publishing.

The problems associated with writing the history of Muhammad are covered in the following:

Peters, F (1991). The quest of the historical Muhammad, *International Journal of Middle East Studies, 23*(3), 291-315.

Donner, FM (1998). *Narratives of Islamic origins: The beginnings of Islamic historical writing.* Princeton, NJ: The Darwin Press.

Moving to the life and history of Muhammad more specifically, from a huge repertoire, the following can be recommended:

Armstrong, K (1992). *Muhammad: A biography of the Prophet.* San Francisco: Harper.

Bearman, P et al (2014) *Encyclopaedia of Islam.* Leiden: Brill Online.

Bennett, C (1998). *In search of Muhammad.* London: Continuum International Publishing Group.

Brockopp, J (Ed), (2010). *The Cambridge companion to Muhammad.* London: Cambridge University Press.

Esposito, J (third ed 2004). *Islam, the straight path.* Oxford: Oxford University Press.

Esposito, J (second ed, 2011). *What everyone needs to know about Islam.* Oxford: Oxford University Press.

Nigosian, SA (2004). *Islam: Its history, teaching, and practices.* Bloomington, IN: Indiana University Press.

Peters, F (1994) *Muhammad and the origins of Islam.* New York: SUNY Press.

Peters, F (2003). *Islam.* Princeton, NJ: Princeton University Press.

Peters, F (2004). *The children of Abraham.* Princeton, NJ: Princeton University Press.

Shoemaker, S. (2001). *The death of a Prophet: The end of Muhammad's life and the beginnings of Islam.* Philadelphia: University of Pennsylvania Press.

Watt WM (1974). *Muhammad: Prophet and statesman.* Oxford: Oxford University Press.

Watt, WM (1953). *Muhammad at Mecca.* Oxford: Clarendon Press.

Zeitlin, I (2007). *The historical Muhammad.* New York: John Wiley & Sons.

5
The Qur'an as a Source of Truth for Islamic Thought And Practice

It is of importance to see where Islam, in the past and present, turns for its theology and sacred practice. This source can be summed up as the Muslim knowledge enshrined in the *shari'ah*, the Law of Islam. We have already mentioned the Qur'an, the Recitation of Muhammad, and we will now examine this as the main source of sacred knowledge in Islam.

No-one can appreciate Islam unless they can understand the pivotal role of the Qur'an and the *shari'ah* in the life of the Muslim.

Theology, Morality and the Qur'an

Islam continued to attract new populations. The religion was simple enough: Muslims were those who submitted themselves to Allah. That submission had to be put into practice. The Muslim had to know therefore what was right and what was wrong. This was achieved by adherence to the *shari'ah* or 'pathway'. This is sometimes called the Law of Islam but it is more than a legal system. According to the prevailing theology, *shari'ah* regulates the Muslim's entire life, not only in matters of public order but also in matters of private morality, etiquette, hygiene and religious ritual. The *shari'ah* shows how the individual Muslim can achieve the status of submission to Allah, be pleasing to Allah and worthy of a happy future beyond death. The pressing need for a Muslim of any time is to understand how the *shari'ah*, as a Pathway, can be known in detail. The most important source for this knowledge has always been the Qur'an.

Traditionally, the Muslim belief has been that the final collection of the Qur'an was achieved under Abu Bakr, the first Caliph, or successor to Muhammad. Four editions circulated and, as we saw above, under 'Uthman, the third Caliph, these were reduced to one authorised version, with all other existing ones being destroyed (n.b. the consequent controversial nature of the recent discovery of Qur'anic fragments spoken about in the previous chapter). The authorised version then became the genuine Arabic copy of the dictation to Muhammad, as we have it today.

The Make-up and Place of the Qur'an

The Qur'an consists of 114 surahs or chapters, unequal in length. Its arrangement does not follow any obvious order. The longer surahs are placed at the beginning (even though they are usually attributed to the period after Muhammad's move to Medina) and the shorter ones towards the end (even though they are usually attributed to the earlier period of Muhammad's preaching in Mecca). The earlier ones tend to be of a more aggressive character. The later ones are written in a more fluent style and the legal content increases, probably indicating the time of organisation and direction of early Muslim communities as they developed and matured.

We will now see the contribution of the Qur'an to the *shari'ah*.

Examining the contents of the Qur'an, the reader is struck by the often repeated affirmation that Allah is one, and only he is to be worshipped. The worst sin that a person can commit is *shirk,* which means associating Allah with other beings or giving Allah a divine partner.[1] In order to avoid any semblance of idol worship, Muslims have forbidden the use of statues, images and pictures in any religious setting. Their mosques and other places of worship are remarkable for their artistic austerity with geometric designs or flower symbols constituting the only decoration.

Again and again, the Qur'an makes mention of the Last Day and Allah's role as Judge, dispensing rewards and punishments. Muhammad saw it as one of his prime duties to remind the new believers that the One God was a Judge. At the same time, Allah had been described as merciful and forgiving. Each surah in the Qur'an, except one, begins in this way:

> In the Name of Allah, the Compassionate, the Merciful....

The Qur'an upholds the former tribal *muruwwa*. However, Muslims are called to see themselves not just as members of a local tribe but as part of the *Ummah*, the vast Muslim world; the *Ummah* has replaced the many tribes out of which the Muslims had come. The Qur'an nonetheless continues the tribal ethical system of hospitality, equity and just dealing and applied it to the whole *Ummah* of Islam.

There were, however, restrictions on earlier tribal ethics. Among the tribes, responsibility for exacting vengeance had belonged to the kinship group of the victim, and responsibility for the crime fell on the culprit's kinship group. Sometimes tribal law had allowed for a substitution for manslaughter and even for murder. For example, a number of camels might be substituted for the life of a guilty person. This was not, however, a fixed rule and some tribes would not countenance it, particularly in the case of murder. The Qur'an encouraged the parties to accept substitution in all cases:

> O you who believe! retaliation is prescribed for you in the matter of the slain, the free for the free, and the slave for

---

1. It is for this reason that Islam has always been suspicious of the Christian doctrine of the Trinity, that there are three persons in the one divine being, a teaching that Islam interprets as giving The Father two partners.

> the slave, and the female for the female, but if any pardon is made to any one by the aggrieved party, then prosecution [for the bloodshed] should be made according to usage, and payment should be made to the aggrieved party in a good manner; this is an alleviation from your Lord and a mercy; so whoever exceeds the limit after this he shall have a painful chastisement.
>
> *Surah 2: 178*

However, in the case of accidental death or manslaughter, substitution was made obligatory:

> And it does not behoove a believer to kill a believer, except by mistake, and whoever kills a believer by mistake, he in turn should free a believing slave, and blood-money should be paid to his people unless they remit it as alms; but if he be from a tribe hostile to you and he is a believer, the freeing of a believing slave suffices, and if he is from a tribe between whom and you there is a covenant, the blood-money should be paid to his people along with the freeing of a believing slave; but he who cannot find a slave should fast for two months successively: a penance from Allah, and Allah is Knowing, Wise.
>
> *Surah 4:92*

It is clear that, here and in other instances, the ethical stance of the Qur'an is somewhere between the ways of the earlier tribal societies and the new individualism found in a commercial society like Mecca. While the law of retaliation still stood, there was a stress on individual responsibility. However, it is made quite clear that everyone would have to answer for their deeds on the Day of Judgement.

Another new development in the Qur'an was the need for forgiveness. This was not a virtue highly prized by tribal mores; indeed, it would have been seen as a weakness. In contrast, the Qur'an requires mercy and forgiveness and good works; these are not a sign of weakness but of strength, the strength that results from submission to Allah:

> And obey Allah and the Apostle [Muhammad], that you may be shown mercy.

> And hasten to forgiveness from your Lord; and a Paradise, the extensiveness of which covers the heavens and the earth, is prepared for those who guard against evil.
> Those who give alms in good times and in bad, and those who restrain their anger and pardon others. Allah loves the charitable.
>
> *Surah* 3:134

The Qur'an also contains something similar to the Ten Commandments of Judaism (which were later re-used in Christianity):

> Do not associate with Allah any other god, lest you sit down despised, neglected.
> And your Lord has commanded that you shall not serve any but Him.
>
> Show kindness to your parents. If either or both of them reach old age with you, do not be impatient with them or rebuke them. Speak to them a generous word.
> And treat them with humility and be gentle to them with compassion, and say: O my Lord! have compassion on them', They nursed me when I was little.
>
> Your Lord knows best what is in your minds; if you are good, then He is surely forgiving to those who turn to Him frequently.
>
> And give to your dependents what they require and give to the needy and the wayfarer, and do not squander wastefully. Surely the squanderers are on the side of Shaitan [Satan] and the Shaitan is ever ungrateful to his Lord.
> And if you need to turn away from them, then since you seek mercy from your Lord, which you hope for, then speak to them a gentle word.
> And do not be a miser or a spendthrift. The former would bring you a reproach and the latter would bring you to poverty.
>
> Surely your Lord gives abundantly to those whom He pleases and He gives sparingly to others. He knows and watches over his servants.

And do not kill your children for fear of poverty; we will provide for them and you too; surely to kill them is a great wrong.

You shall not commit adultery; surely it is an indecency and an evil way.

And do not kill any one whom Allah has forbidden you to kill, except for a just cause. If a person is killed unjustly, that person's heir is entitled to some return. The heir should not revenge the unjust death since the victim then will, in turn, be avenged.

And do not interfere with the property of the orphan except in a good way until the orphan attains maturity and fulfills your promise; you must give an account of every promise.

And give full measure when you measure out, and weigh with just scales; this is fair and will work better in the end.

And follow not that of which you have not the knowledge; surely the hearing and the sight and the heart, all of these, shall be questioned.

And do not go proudly in the land, for you cannot open up the earth nor reach the mountains in height.

All this is evil and is hateful in the sight of your Lord.

Surah 17:22-38

Not only in this catalogue cited above, but in other texts as well, the Qur'an answers many of the ethical questions that life continually throws up for the Muslim. Following various texts in the Qur'an, the Muslim would know, among other things, the following:

Q. Must I honour and worship Allah?
A. Absolutely
Q. Can I give a partner to Allah (as for example the other two persons in the Christian Trinity)?
A. Absolutely not
Q. Can I retaliate if someone deliberately kills one of my family?

A. Yes, but it is better to come to a merciful arrangement.
Q. Can I retaliate if someone accidentally kills one of my family?
A. No. But you can require blood-money.
Q. Should I show mercy to other people?
A. Absolutely
Q. Should I be kind to my parents?
A. Yes. If circumstances do not allow caring for them, be gentle to them.
Q. Should I care for my dependants?
A. Yes, and also for the needy in general. Once again, if impossible, be gentle.
Q. Can I squander my goods as I like?
A. No. And do not be a miser with your goods either.
Q. Can I kill my children if poverty becomes dire?
A. Absolutely not.
Q. Can I commit adultery?
A. Absolutely not.
Q. Do I need to look after orphans?
A. Yes, they need protection and their inherited property must be respected.
Q. Do I have to be just in my commercial dealings?
A. Yes
Q. Can I take on airs and graces in my demeanour?
A. Absolutely not. You are not as important as you may think. While the Qur'an is the principal source for the Islamic *shari'ah*, it does not cover all the circumstances of life in detail. A new source was required to give ethical direction on questions that had no answer in the Qur'an, often brought about by new situations not foreseen at the time of its writing. The second source was called the *Sunnah*, or the 'custom' of Muhammad and we now turn to that in the next chapter.

Notes:

Further information can be found in the following:

Bearman, P et al (sec ed, 2014). *Encyclopaedia of Islam*, Leiden: Brill Online.
Esposito, J (third ed, 2004). *Islam, the straight path*, Oxford: Oxford University Press.

Grieve, P (2006). *Islam—history, faith and politics: The complete introduction*. London: Robinson.

Lovat, T (2005). The scriptural evidence of Islam: Ramifications for Judaism and Christianity. *Religious Education Journal of Australia, 21*, 3-11.

Lovat, T (2006). Interpreting the scriptures of Islam and implications for the West. *International Journal of the Humanities, 4*, 63-69.

Lovat, T (2006). Islam as the religion of 'fair go': An important lesson for Australian religious education. *Journal of Religious Education, 54*, 49-53.

Lovat, T (2010). Islam and ethics. In M Gray & S Webb (Eds), *Ethics and value perspectives in social work* (pp 298-314). London: Palgrave.

Nasr, S (2002). *The heart of Islam*. San Francisco: Harper.

Pedry, A (2010). *Methods of Qur'anic analysis: A comparison of Islamic and Western*. http://www.suite101com/content/methods-of-quranic-analysis-a-comparison-of-islamic-and-western-a299353#ixzz1FmdTOqTf. (Accessed 19 June 2013)

6
The *Sunnah* of Muhammad

The Qur'an was not, and still is not, the only source for sacred knowledge and life-direction among the Muslims. They have looked also to Tradition. We may recall that the main issue at the time of the Christian Reformation was: is sacred Christian knowledge contained in the Bible alone or also in the Tradition that had been handed on in the work of later authoritative writers and particularly the Pope of Rome? This question caused great divisions among Christians and brought about the Reformation.

In Islam, in somewhat the same way, the Qur'an was seen as an infallible and divine book, but other sources were acknowledged as providing sacred knowledge as well.

These other sources are summed up in the title, the Sunnah of Muhammad.

The Origins and Make-up of the Sunnah

The *Sunnah* of Muhammad was composed of a string of *hadiths* or 'traditions'. These related many of the actions and sayings of Muhammad; they were mostly biographical items. They could vary in importance. One *hadith* told of Muhammad's reaction when a baby wet him; another promoted cleaning teeth after a meal. In contrast, others addressed more profound human matters; they even took on a fantastic tone at times. For example, Muhammad was said to have received messages from camels and to have healed his wounded soldiers instantaneously. These traditions had been handed on by word of mouth and they consisted of a *matn* or 'text' and an *isnad* or 'foundation'. A particular tradition's authority could be gauged by its chain of transmitters, making up the *isnad*: A told me that B said that C had informed him that D related that he heard E say that he heard F ask the Apostle of Allah about ……..

These *isnad*s ensured that Muhammad's authority would be brought into the present. The present could be constructed and reconstructed on the past. The *hadiths* preserved the life teaching of Muhammad as an exemplar.

During the centuries after the death of Muhammad, there was wide dissemination of these *hadiths*. They were not only sayings and examples from the life of Muhammad, but they also included precedents established by the first four Caliphs and the statements of the Companions of Muhammad, said to be the first believers in Mecca. There was also the occasional legitimate fabrication; Muslims with a cause felt free to invent a *hadith* to support their position. Hence, in time, there was the problem of distinguishing true and false *hadiths*.

The way of managing this was through examination of the *isnads*, or foundations. Muslim scholars in the ninth century CE undertook the work and gathered *hadiths* from around the world of Islam. They were subjected to scrutiny and each *hadith* was declared sound, good or weak in descending order. From this scrutiny, there emerged six collections of *hadiths* known as the Six Sound Books. They contained a few thousand of what would have been hundreds of thousands of *hadiths* in circulation.

Islamic interpreters discovered, however, that even after scrutinising the Qur'an and the Sunnah, there could still be doubt about the right way of living in some particular instances. In this case, the Muslim would have to consult the *'ijma* or 'consensus' of the past generations of Muslims. This would be expressed in the public opinion of the Muslim community and given voice by Islamic jurists when they agreed on the rightness or wrongness of some human activity.

Only when these three sources for the *shari'ah* failed to produce a satisfying answer, could the Muslim turn to the last resort—*Qiyas* or 'analogy'. *Qiyas* established a parallel between a teaching that had been already well established (from the Qur'an or the *hadiths* or *'ijma*) and applied it to a new set of circumstances. It moved from the known, where the ethical issue had been solved, to the unknown for which it provided a clear analogy.

Thus, for example, the Qur'an clearly prohibited the drinking of alcohol because of its intoxicating effects including, in particular, the disturbance it caused during prayer to Allah. The prohibition is clear enough in the Qur'an:

> O you who believe! Intoxicants and games of chance and sacrificing to stones set up and dividing by arrows are only an uncleanness, the Shaitan's work; shun it therefore that you may be successful.
> The Shaitan only desires to cause enmity and hatred to spring in your midst by means of intoxicants and games of chance, and to keep you off from the remembrance of Allah and from prayer. Will you then desist?
>
> *Surah 5:90-91*

And there is another passage:

> They ask you about intoxicants and games of chance. Say: In both of them there is a great sin and means of profit for men, and their sin is greater than their profit. And they ask you as to what they should spend. Say: What you can spare. Thus does Allah make clear to you the communications that you may ponder.
>
> *Surah 2:219*

The connection between intoxication and the inability to pray is made clear in a text that deals with the right preparations for prayer:

> O you who believe! do not go near prayer when you are intoxicated until you know well what you say, nor when you are under an obligation to perform a bath - unless you are travelling on the road - until you have washed yourselves; and if you are sick, or on a journey, or one of you come from the privy or you have touched women, and you cannot find water, betake yourselves to pure earth, then wipe your faces and your hands; surely Allah is pardoning and forgiving.

Surah 4:43

For the vast majority of Muslims, this is positive proof that the *shari'ah* bans the drinking of alcohol (even if some Muslims might not adhere to the prohibition). What then do we make of taking illicit drugs for recreational use? The Qur'an and the Sunnah have nothing explicitly to say. Many maintain furthermore that the consensus of scholars has never been clear on this matter. On the other hand, most Muslims would claim, on the basis of *qiyas* or analogy, that if Muhammad banned alcohol because it could interfere with the cycle of required prayers, then he would have banned illicit drugs as well.

Of course, in this case, as in others, it could be that if enough scholars agreed on this point of *qiyas*, it could acquire the stronger authority of *'ijma*.

Hence, the *shari'ah* can be established as to its ethical requirements with sufficient accuracy to satisfy most Muslims. In the mosques and in religious texts, Muslim preachers and writers consider themselves empowered to determine what is right and what is wrong. These mandates are not considered to be human inventions; they carry the authority of Muhammad speaking through the Qur'an, the Sunnah, *'ijma* and *qiyas*.

When the Muslim looks to discover the *shari'ah*, or Pathway to Allah, then there are apt directions regarding individual, social and political moral behaviours. There is justice tempered with mercy and forgiveness, truthfulness, sexual integrity, honesty and compassion for other humans. All human activity, based on the sources, is able to be divided by Muslim jurists into five categories. Any individual action can be classified as obligatory, recommended, permitted, disapproved but not forbidden, or absolutely forbidden.

Having seen the duties directed towards the believing community and the world of humanity that surrounds the Muslim, we can look at those duties more directed towards Allah himself. These are called the Five Pillars of Islam.

Notes

See Notes for chapters 3 and 5 especially.

7
The Five Pillars of Islam

From what has been written, the *shari'ah* can therefore be determined according to the methods of Muslim ethicists. Beyond constituting the list of laws incumbent on Muslims, the *shari'ah* is also the essential component of Muslim life, etched into its fabric.

In fact, there is no aspect of Muslim life that is not touched by *shari'ah*.

The meaning of *muslim*, as we have seen, is 'submission'. *Shari'a* requires that this submission, the essential focus of all Islam, should be made manifest in the life pattern of the Muslim.

The Muslim must carry out a life practice in accordance with the *Shari'a*; but the Muslim also has commitments to Allah. The Muslim, above all else, must demonstrate absolute submission to Allah.

Hence, there is a requirement on all Muslims to follow the Five Pillars, five basic practices by which the Muslims demonstrate such absolute submission and surrender to Allah in faithful action.

We will deal in turn with each of what have become known as the Five Pillars of Islam. These are essential to the true religious practice of all Muslims.

The First Pillar

The first pillar is the *shahadah* or 'profession of faith'. This is the proclamation that Allah is God above all things and that Muhammad is his prophet: 'There is no God but Allah, and Muhammad is his Prophet'. This has become the rallying call of Islam; its announcement to the world is made (when possible and allowed) five times a day from the mosque's tower or minaret. These are the first words whispered into the ear of a new-born; they are the words spoken to a person on their death-bed. The profession of faith occurs many times in the Qur'an.

The Second Pillar

The second pillar is *salat* or 'prayer'. This is not a reference to prayer in general; it is a particular, very physical type of prayer. The text for recital and the accompanying actions are laid down by strict tradition. Five times a day (dawn, noon, afternoon, evening and night), the Muslim is required to face towards Mecca and, either alone or in a congregation (preferably in a mosque), to go through a ritual of movement and prayer that expresses both in words and in actions a complete surrender to Allah. The Qur'an explains this ritual with its precise bowings and prostrations:

> And when you are among the believers and keep up the prayer for them, let a party of them stand up with you, and let them put aside their arms; then when they have prostrated themselves let them go to your rear, and let another party who have not prayed come forward and pray with you, and let them take their precautions and their arms; for those who disbelieve desire that you may be careless of your arms and your luggage, so that they may then turn upon you with a sudden united attack, and there is no blame on you, if you are annoyed with rain or if you are sick, that you lay down your arms, and take your precautions; surely Allah has prepared a disgraceful chastisement for the unbelievers. Then when you

have finished the prayer, remember Allah standing and sitting and reclining; but when you are secure [from danger] keep up prayer; surely prayer is a timed ordinance for the believers.

Surah 4:102-103

The Third Pillar

The same submission to Allah is expressed in the third pillar: *zakat* or 'almsgiving'. The Qur'an reads:

> And We made them Imams who guided [people] by Our command, and We revealed to them the doing of good and the keeping up of prayer and the giving of the alms, and Us [alone] did they serve;

Surah 21: 73

A proportion of the Muslim's income is deducted to support the Islamic community. The proportion of earnings is usually determined in modern Muslim communities as 2.5% of income. However, this exact determination is not found in the Qur'an; it is found in the *hadiths*. This religious tax can be used for the upkeep of holy places and mosques or for the relief of the poor and needy. Muslims are also separately required to assist the needy poor who beg in the streets.

The Fourth Pillar

The fourth pillar is *sawm* or 'fasting' during the holy month of Ramadan. The Qur'an is explicit in its details concerning the holy fast:

> The month of Ramadan is that in which the Quran was revealed, a guidance to men and clear proofs of the guidance and the distinction of Allah; therefore whoever of you is present in the month shall fast therein, and whoever is sick or upon a journey shall fast an equal number of other days; Allah desires ease for you, and He does not desire for you difficulty, and He desires that you should complete the number of days and that you should exalt the greatness of Allah for His having guided you and that you may give thanks.

> It is made lawful to you to go into your wives on the night of the fast; they are a comfort to you and you are a comfort to them; Allah knew that you had deceived yourselves, so He has mercifully turned to you and removed this burden from you; so now be in contact with them and seek what Allah has ordained for you, and eat and drink until the whiteness of the day becomes distinct from the blackness of the night at dawn, then complete the fast till night, and have no contact with them but stay in the mosques; these are the limits set by Allah, so do not go near them. Thus does Allah make clear His communications to believers that they may guard against evil.
>
> *Surah* 2:185, 187

The determination of the date of Ramadan is based on the lunar calendar, long used by Muslims. The calendar's first day is based on the *hijra* of Muhammad from Mecca to Medina. Because it is lunar, any date, compared to the Western calendar, will advance in the yearly seasons as time goes by. Ramadan can therefore occur sometimes in summer, sometimes in winter. During Ramadan, from dawn to sunset, the Muslim is required to abstain from eating, drinking (even water), sexual intercourse and smoking. After sunset and before dawn, they can eat and drink and have marital intercourse as normal.

In some Muslim countries, the decision over the beginning and end of Ramadan is made by a Muslim official determining when a white thread and a black thread can no longer be distinguished (sunset) and then when a white thread and a black thread can be distinguished (sunrise). At this time, a cannon was often fired to alert the Muslim populace to the beginning and end of the day's fast.

The Ramadan fast ends with the festival of 'Id-ul-Fitr, or Eid (Festival of the Breaking [of the fast]) which lasts for three days. On the first day, there is a prayer meeting in the mosque and the head of each family distributes alms for the needy. Presents are often given to children. Over the three days, the opportunity is taken to visit or contact Muslim friends.

The Fifth Pillar

The final Pillar is *Hajj* or 'pilgrimage'. Once in a lifetime, all Muslims, male and female, are required to make the sacred journey to Mecca and its surrounds during the twelfth month of the lunar calendar. This obligation is dependent on the ability, physical and economic, of the particular Muslim. In Mecca, they should perform a ritual that recalls the beginnings of Islam. The ritual consists of travelling to Mecca and arriving clothed only in two white sheets. All pilgrims are indistinguishable by dress; any garments that indicate class or superiority are not allowed; all Muslims making the Hajj are equal.

The pilgrims visit the Ka'aba, the sacred cube, in the centre of the Mosque which was cleansed of its false gods by Muhammad, and perform a sevenfold circular walk around it. Then the pilgrims await the beginning of the official ceremonies. After prayers at the Ka'aba, the pilgrims go out to an extensive plain called Arafat, about twenty-four kilometres from Mecca. There they perform the 'standing' ceremony, during which they listen to a sermon which commemorates the Farewell Sermon of Muhammad to his people, delivered on this plain during the last year of his life.

On the return journey, the people stop at a small town called Mina, where there are three stone pillars that represent *Shaitan* (Satan), who originated all evil. They throw seven pebbles at these pillars to show their disdain for *Shaitan*, and then return to Mecca for the final ceremonies. After once more going around the Ka'aba, the pilgrims leave Mecca. The *Hajj* ritual is designed to re-present the founding experience of Islam by Muhammad in Mecca. By following in the footsteps of Muhammad, the believing group hopes to experience the enlightenment that came to him when he was in the presence of Allah.

It is often asked: was this the exact ground-plan of Muhammad's founding movements? Regardless of the answer, how much does it really matter for the believers taking part in this celebration, for most of them on their first and only trip to the most sacred site of Islam?

Although the rituals of the *Hajj* have developed over time, the actual notion of the *Hajj* already appeared in the Qur'an:

> When We assigned to Ibrahim the site for the House [the Ka'aba], saying: Do not associate Me with any other, and

purify My House for those who make the circuit and stand to pray and bow and prostrate themselves.

And proclaim among men the Hajj [the Pilgrimage]: the believers will come to you on foot and on every lean camel, coming from every remote quarter, they will come to avail themselves of many benefits and mention the name of Allah during the stated days over the cattle he has given them. Eat of them and feed the distressed ones and the needy.

Then let them accomplish their needful acts of shaving and cleansing, and let them fulfil their vows and let them encircle the Ancient House.

Surah 22:27-29

These Five Pillars or rituals of Islam encompass the constant need for submission to Allah in the lives of all Muslims. Through them, the Muslim constantly acts out absolute submission to Allah in ritual activity.

Notes

See Notes for chapters 3 and 5 especially.

8
The Early Divisions of Islam

So far, we have been speaking of Islam as a monolith, as if there was one Islamic community worldwide and none other. That might or might not have been true in its very earliest days, but, as we suggested in the Preface to this book, it was not to be the experience of later history.

Islam is a study in difference as much as commonality.

As far as we can tell, early Islam tended to be fairly authoritarian, as often happens when a new community is forming around a set of particular beliefs and ideals. It was based on submission and this submission was etched into the life of the individual Muslim. These earliest Muslims, by whatever name, might have expected that the unity would continue beyond the time of its foundation, including beyond the death of Muhammad.

The death of Muhammad raised the question of succession. Who would be the leader after Muhammad?

The first principle of succession, as recorded in the foundation story from some centuries later, namely that the Caliphs, or Muhammad's deputies, had to be blood relatives of Muhammad, would have seemed to guarantee unity. In fact, neither this principle nor anything else guaranteed anything like unity, and division has been a characteristic of Islam from its earliest days to the present day.

The Spread and Fracturing of Islam

According to the foundation story, when Muhammad died in 632 CE, he left no immediate successor. By default, the Muslim society was led by Muhammad's father-in-law, Abu Bakr, who took the title of *Khalif* or 'Deputy'. The English form is Caliph. This was something like the belief that Peter succeeded Jesus in Christianity. Abu Bakr was cast in the story as a veteran, one of the Companions of the Prophet Muhammad. He had accompanied Muhammad from Mecca to Medina and Muhammad was married to his daughter, A'isha, his third wife. Under Abu Bakr's leadership, Islam continued to spread.

Islam's armies moved into Syria, Palestine, Iraq, Persia and Egypt. By 636 CE, all of Syria and Palestine were in Islamic hands except for Jerusalem and Caesarea. One Caliph succeeded another. Abu Bakr died in 634 CE and was succeeded by 'Umar (634-644 CE), a brother-in-law to Muhammad, and then 'Uthman (644-656 CE), a son-in-law. Under 'Umar there was further Islamic expansion as far as Damascus, and Jerusalem became a Muslim city. 'Umar found in Egypt a battleground between the native Copts and the Byzantine Greeks. In 640 CE, the Byzantines were overrun, with the Islamic armies often assisted by the Copts.

Although under 'Uthman there was some further expansion to the borders of Afghanistan and along the North African coast, he was considered weak and disunity was beginning to show.

According to the story, the fourth successor of Muhammad was 'Ali, Muhammad's cousin and son-in-law, who had married Fatima, Muhammad's daughter by his first wife, Khadija. It was said that 'Ali had converted to Islam at the age of nine. It was now thirty years since Muhammad had died and the four successors—Abu Bakr, 'Umar, 'Uthman and 'Ali—would be known as the *Rashidun* or the 'Rightly Guided Ones'. The earlier signs of disunity however became more and more apparent as time went by.

'Ali was forced into a struggle for power with the Muslim governor of Syria, Mu'awiya of the Umayyad tribe. These Umayyads belonged to the Quraysh, the consortium of tribes from which Muhammad himself had originated, but the Umayyads were despots, whose observance of Islam was said to be lax. In a battle at Siffin on the Euphrates River in 657 CE, an indecisive 'Ali is said to have submitted to arbitration over the issue of the succession of a Caliph. Some of his adherents considered this to be a betrayal of Islam. For them, only Allah could arbitrate about such an issue; they believe that 'Ali's followers should have continued to fight.

These discontented followers seceded from his rule. One of the Kharijites or 'Seceders' assassinated 'Ali, and so the Umayyad Mu'awiya became the new Caliph. According to the story, it was 661 CE and the era of the Rashidun had come to an end. So it was that the mainstream Muslim world was ruled and organised from Damascus under Umayyad Caliphs for a considerable time, up to 750 CE. The expansion of Islam under these Umayyad rulers would reach as far as Spain.

The Umayyad dynasty saw a need for a new basis for the Islamic world that they had inherited. It would not be built on the theocracy or God-rule of Islam but on Arab secular rule. This stance would by no means please all Muslims. There would be further splits.

Major Division in Islam: Sunnis and Shia

After this first major rift in Islam took place, there were those who accepted the Umayyad Caliphs, and those who considered that a Caliph must continue to be a direct descendant of Muhammad.

The former group became known as the Sunnis, from *Ahl al-Sunna* or 'people of the tradition'. They have followed only the Qur'an and the *Sunnah*. For them, Muhammad was the last and greatest of the prophets. They looked back to the four Rightly Guided Caliphs, the Rashidun, with great reverence. However, any subsequent leader of Islam (such as an Umayyad leader) was seen as a temporal figure, not carrying the authority of Muhammad and the Rashidun.

Sunni Islam, regarded as the more traditional division, maintains that all knowledge from Allah and all direction about how to live a good Muslim life ceased with the death of Muhammad and the writing of the Qur'an. There was only a need to elaborate and apply those principles to new situations, and this was the purpose of the *Sunnah* and its *hadiths*.

Up to modern times, the majority of Muslims have been Sunnis and have followed the lead of the Qur'an and the *Sunnah* of Muhammad as it was handed down from the past. Allowing for sub-groups, Sunni

Islam is said to account for 75% to 90% of the present-day Islamic population.

The second group adhered to the deceased 'Ali's sons, Hassan and al-Husain, and became known as the *Shiat 'Ali* or 'party of 'Ali'. Hence, they are usually called Shi'ites or Shia Muslims. They insisted that 'Ali, as a relative of Muhammad, and his descendants should be the only acceptable leaders of the Islamic *ummah*. However, both of 'Ali's sons died; Hassan was probably dispatched by poison organised by Mu'awiya, and al-Husain was killed in battle.

From the beginnings of the division from Sunni Islam, and through until the present day, a major annual celebration for Shia Islam is the celebration of the anniversary of the death of al-Husain, killed by the Sunnis and an event still burning deep in the psyche of the Shi'ites. Religious processions at the celebration typically incorporate a representation of al-Husain's tomb, a horse covered with a bloodstained cover and with arrows fixed in its harness, and a display of self-flagellation by devotees. The Passion of al-Husain is the major festival of the Shi'ite year and his shrine at Karbala is regarded as sacred ground. Karbala is about 100 kilometres southwest of Baghdad in Iraq, and was the site for the battle during which al-Husain was killed.

In contrast to the Sunnis, Shia Islam holds that further divine guidance remains available through the descendants of Muhammad, known as imams or 'leaders'. In Iran, some of these have become known as Ayatollahs or 'Signs of Allah', imams who are marked out by their wide Islamic study and holiness. These ayatollahs could reveal, without possibility of any error, the inner meaning of the Qur'an and could actually add to the original revelation from Allah. This is ongoing and still applies today, showing how it is that an Ayatollah like Ruhollah Khomeini, the leader of the 1979 Iranian Revolution in Iran, could be the subject of such religious awe. His Shi'ite followers could truly see Allah revealing a new set of commands suited to the needs of the time being channeled through his person.

What was achieved by the *'ijma* or consensus of Islam among the Sunnis was replaced by the infallible decisions of the imam and ayatollah among the Shia. This point of difference between Sunni and Shia Islam requires some comment.

Sunni Islam does not place emphasis on sacred persons; its main emphasis is on the book, the Qur'an. The imams who preside over Sunni prayer sessions, for example, are not indispensable and can be readily replaced by others, if there is need. Likewise, the *katib* or 'preacher' in the Sunni mosque is simply a learned and devout Muslim who expatiates on the Qur'an. He does not add to it; he explains it. The muezzin is the person charged with calling the Sunni Muslims to prayer by singing from the top of a minaret, if it exists; this is an office and the muezzin is not distinguished by any added holiness.

The situation is different in Shia Islam. Shia maintains that in every generation there should be an infallible imam, a Grand Ayatollah. This man is charged with the task of declaring the meaning of the Qur'an and its ramifications in more modern circumstances to the people of his time. Hence, Shia Islam places much greater stock on its sacred persons than does Sunni Islam.

The principal difference therefore between Sunni and Shia Islam is that Sunni Islam looks back to the Qur'an and its official interpretation in the Six Sound Books of *hadiths,* whereas Shia Islam believes that an officially recognised imam has authority over the community of Islam and can make contemporary decisions about Islamic belief and practice. This difference in theology has continued to impact on Islam from its earliest days through to the present.

As already suggested, about 10% to 20% of modern Muslims belong to Shia Islam.

On both sides of this major split within Islam, the emotion and hostility felt towards the other is probably deeper and more long-standing than the deepest split in Christianity between Catholicism and Protestantism[1]. Nonetheless, the bitterness between Catholics and Protestants during the Reformation, or even more recently in Northern Ireland, would shed some light on the depth of feelings between Sunni and Shia Muslims.

We will now look at the Sufis, another Muslim breakaway.

---

1. The division of Roman Catholics and Protestants is also similar to the Sunni and Shia division. Broadly speaking, Protestants maintain that the Bible contains all divine teaching and practice; Roman Catholics maintain that the Bible as interpreted by the Church (mainly the Pope) provides new divine teaching and practice.

The Sufis

The split between Sunni and Shia Islam was not the only significant division in the founding years. There had always been a tendency amongst some Muslims towards mysticism. Mysticism describes an ecstatic encounter with the divinity, in which the divinity connects with the individual directly instead of indirectly through sacred persons, sacred places, religious rituals and sacred stories. It might seem that Islam would be exempt from such familiarity and intimacy with Allah, since it stressed the utter distance of humans from Allah and saw the principal religious need to be absolute submission and adherence to the Qur'an.

However, in the time after the Umayyads had seized control of mainstream Islam, many Muslims (besides the Shia) became disenchanted with the worldliness and luxury of the court of the Sunni Caliphs. They reacted to the many political and religious dissensions that seemed to pull the Islamic world apart. They were not satisfied with the arid Muslim piety that was being practised. Accordingly, from about a century after the establishment of Islam, certain believers sought a more personal and spiritual way of Muslim life.

An ascetic Muslim movement began in Iraq. Its members became known as Sufis, probably because their members wore a coarse *suf* or woolen garment. The Sufis showed great contempt for the political world with its pleasures and power-games and they spent their time repeating litanies containing phrases such as 'Allah' or 'There is no God but Allah' over and over again or being involved in rhythmic dancing. This repetitive form of prayer or dancing was known as *dhikr* or 'remembering'. The Sufis felt that by performing such ritual they were able to come into the presence of Allah directly. A new religious spirit developed separately from Sunni Islam and Shia Islam, although existing on the fringes of both.

This religious spirit is exemplified in the words of a female Sufi poet, Rabia al-Adawiya (who died in 801 CE), describing her relationship with Allah in terms of selfless love:

> I love you with two loves, love of my happiness
> And perfect love, to love you as is your due.

> My selfish love is that I do nothing
> But think on you, excluding all else beside;
> But the purest love, which is your due,
> Is that the veils which hid you fall, and I gaze on you.
> (cited in Fadiman & Frager, 1997:86)

This ascetic mysticism of the Sufis, renouncing the pleasures of the world, gave birth to a more ardent love for Allah, who had seemed so distant in the courts of the Umayyads. Sufis wanted to be at one with Allah, to know him personally like a friend and the *dhikrs* were techniques used to accomplish this intimate union. Whereas Sunni Islam and Shia Islam aimed more at absolute submission to Allah, the Sufis aimed more at personal union with him in a loving relationship. This is not to say that the Sufis did not esteem submission or that the Sunnis and Shi'ites knew nothing of divine love.

For the first three centuries, Sufism was practised in small groups or individually. There were no congregational features within the movement. Gradually, the Sufis became more cautious. Their writings used veiled and symbolic language for what they believed. They became more or less reconciled with the more mainstream forms of Islam, although the *Ummah* never officially admitted the validity of a mystical knowledge of Allah.

From the twelfth century CE, communities of Sufis are known to have existed. One of the more famous of these new communities was founded by Jalel ad-Din Rumi, known simply as Rumi (1207-1273 CE). He was given the title of Mevlana or 'Our Teacher' in his native Persia, and he eventually settled in the holy city of Konya, now in modern Turkey. There he established the Dervishes or 'The Poor' (perhaps 'The Beggars'). Their *dhikr* was a highly disciplined dance accompanied by haunting music from a reed pipe. This frenzied dancing ended in ecstasy with the dancers achieving union with Allah. Because of the dancing, they have become known as the Whirling Dervishes.

Just as the Shi'ites looked to the imams and their succession, so the Sufis looked to a leader like Rumi who would guide their mystical lives. This leader or *shaykh* (sheik in English) became the model of how the Muslim life should be led. Divine light was believed to emanate from the sheik. The sheik could demand obedience and trust; sometimes, he would enjoin fasting, silence or solitary meditation on his followers. In this way, it was believed that the lower human instincts of the Sufi could be curbed and the individual Sufi could be filled with Allah-like qualities. An original sheik would nominate a successor and so the Sufi community found continuity.

It is difficult to ascertain a percentage of Sufis in Islam. They do not self-identify as Sufis and they tend to be very secretive because of opposition to them in some Muslim countries[2].

There was an uneasy alliance between the Sufis and Sunni Islam. It could be said that Sufism gave new life to mainstream Islam and endowed it with a more popular appeal. It remains a paradox that the more original authoritarian form of Islam should have consistently generated these forms of individual mysticism. The answer to the paradox is that the Qur'an is a book that is the guardian of orthodoxy but, at the same time, it is the source of mystical vitality.

It needs to be said that at the base of all these forms of Islam – Sunni Islam, Shia Islam and Sufism - lies the account of the revelatory inspiration of Muhammad.

Notes

Most general books on Islam, as cited above in Notes for various chapters, contain extensive accounts of the division of Sunni and Shia Islam. The following are more specific texts:

> Chelkowski, P (Ed), (2010). *Eternal performance: Taziyah and other Shi'ite rituals.* Salt Lake City: Seagull Books.
>
> Dabashi, H (2011). *Shi'ism: A religion of protest.* Cambridge, MA: Harvard University Press.
>
> Halm, H (2004). *Shi'ism.* Edinburgh: Edinburgh University Press.
>
> Halm, H (2007). *The Shi'ites: A short history.* Princeton, NJ: Markus Wiener Publications.
>
> Momen, M (1985). *An introduction to Shi'a Islam: The history and doctrines of Twelver Shi'ism.* New Haven, CT: Yale University Press.

---

2. After World War I, the national leader of Turkey, Mustapha Kemal, wanted to establish his country on a secular basis. He banned the Whirling Dervishes as an embarrassment to a secular culture. Despite this prohibition, the Dervishes have continued to this day.

Nasr, SH & Dabashi, H (1989). *Expectation of the Millennium: Shi'ism in history*. New York: SUNY Press.

Rogerson, B (2007). *The heirs of Muhammad: Islam's first century and the origins of the Sunni Shia split*. New York: Overlook Press.

Wollaston, A (2005). *The Sunnis and Shias*. Whitefish, MT: Kessinger Publishing.

On Sufism and its texts see:

Abun-Nasr, J (2007). *Muslim communities of Grace: The Sufi Brotherhoods in Islamic religious life*. London: Hurst.

Arberry, AJ (1991). *Mystical poems of Rumi, Vols. 1&2*. Chicago: University of Chicago Press.

Dahlén, A (2008). Sufi Islam. In P Clarke & P Beyer (Eds), *The world's religions: Continuities and transformations* (pp 678-695). New York: Routledge.

Fadiman, J & Frager, R (1997). *Rabia, Essential Sufism*. Boulder: Shambhala.

Idries, S (1971). *The Sufis*. New York: Anchor Books.

Schimmel, A (1983). *Mystical dimensions of Islam*. Chapel Hill, NC: University of North Carolina Press.

9
Later Islamic History and More Divisions

The split between Sunni Islam and the Kharijites and then Sunni Islam and Shia Islam were certainly the most dramatic in Islamic history. Sunni and Shi'ite differences still affect world history.

However, as time went by, there would be other divisions, continuing up to today.

We will look at these other divisions and include Islamic State[3] as the most worrying development in the Islamic world today.

Islamic State cannot be studied in isolation. The knowledge about Islam and its divisions acquired so far is necessary to understand what Islamic State is about in the twenty-first century and where it might be leading.

---

3. Islamic State goes under a variety of names. It is sometimes called ISIL (the Islamic State of Iraq and the Levant) and ISIS (the Islamic State of Iraq and Syria) or simply IS for Islamic State. ISIS in Arabic is *ad-Dawlah al-Islāmiyah fī 'l-'Irāq wa-sh-Shām*, leading to the acronym Da'ish, Da'eesh, or DAESH, also used in media descriptions. We will use 'Islamic State' in this text.

The ongoing history of Islam

When the Umayyads took over the Caliphate and made Islam into a dynastic enterprise, the Kharijite movement, Shia Islam and the Sufis each protested for different reasons. In 749 CE, there was a revolution among the Sunnis when Abu al-Abbas was made Caliph in Iraq and defeated the Umayyad Caliph in the following year. This new dynasty was named the Abassid Caliphate after its first father and founder. Its capital was at Baghdad and there was money and leisure for Muslims to indulge in literary and philosophical studies. This was the era in which Islam first began to dominate human education and thought.

There was a further breakaway in 973 CE when the Fatimid Shi'ites (Fatima being the daughter of Muhammad who had married 'Ali) announced that they had appointed their own Caliph and moved their capital to Cairo. Moreover, there was a new force created in the tenth century CE when the Seljuk Turks, a tribal confederation from central Asia, converted to Sunni Islam. By the early eleventh century, the Seljuk Turks had moved into Syria, Palestine and Asia Minor (which had been Byzantine Christian up to that point).

The fall of the Fatimids was brought about by internal weakness. They were replaced by the Ayyubid dynasty, of Kurdish descent, led by a great Muslim warrior, Saladin. Although this dynasty ruled only from 1174-1260 CE, it had tremendous influence. It fostered economic programs, intellectual research and attempted to impose Sunni Islam through the building of religious schools or *madrasas*.

The Ayyubids became decentralised and lost control. The earlier Egyptian Fatimids had had Turkish *mamluks* ('slaves') who were used in their Caliphs' armies and were specially trained in Egypt. The onetime slaves recognised the vacuum, revolted and set up their own Mamluk dynasty in Egypt. This would remain until it crumbled under the Ottomans in the sixteenth century CE.

The political disintegration of Islam and the setting up of puppet Caliphs led to the Islamic world's decay by the eleventh century CE. The Islamic armies were now facing strong Christian attacks – in Spain and in the Crusades[1]. Much more needs to be said about the Crusades.

---

1. The term 'crusade' is a relatively modern term. It was used by later scholars to designate those Europeans who 'took the cross (of Jesus)' and formed an army

During the Crusades, European Christian armies, bearing the emblem of the Christian cross, were sent to the Middle East with the blessing of successive Roman Popes. The Crusades were military campaigns mounted by the Roman Christian Church (as against the Greek Byzantine Church, from which it had been divided since 1054 CE). Pope Urban II convoked the First Crusade in 1095 CE, promising a plenary indulgence to all combatants.[2] The purpose of the First Crusade was to open up access to the holy places in Jerusalem and its environs. Islamic rulers had made it progressively difficult for pilgrims from the West to visit these holy places.

The end result of the First Crusade was the establishment of the Kingdom of Jerusalem in 1099 CE and a number of other Crusader States in the area once held by the Muslims. Other Crusades followed intermittently for the next 200 years. There were great difficulties in maintaining the early gains due to disorder among the diverse elements in the armies, disease and economic problems.

Nine Crusades are named but there were other invasions as well. However, the invasion came to an end in 1291 CE when the Crusader city of Acre was re-taken by the Muslim armies and with that the vision of a Holy Land under the control of the Western Christians came to an end.

This military incursion on the part of Western Christians has caused, as we will see later, great and continuing enmity between the Christian West and Islam.

Islam up to the sixteenth century

In the fourteenth century CE, another Turkish group, the Osmanlis, called the 'Ottomans' in Western Europe, moved against Byzantine Greece. Constantinople fell to Mehmet II in 1453 CE. This was the end of the Byzantine Empire, the Roman Empire in the East. The great Christian basilica of Hagia Sophia in Constantinople, constructed first by Constantine and then magnificently reconstructed by one of his successors, Justinian, became a mosque. The Ottoman sultan, Selim I, assumed the title of Caliph in 1517 CE.

---

of like-minded soldiers to re-take the Holy Land.
2. An indulgence was believed by Roman Christians to remove any future penalty after death for sins committed during life. It did not forgive sins (although that was how many Roman Christians interpreted it), it only remitted the penalties due to sins that had been forgiven. A plenary indulgence removed all penalties.

By this time, the Arabs in the Middle East had been subjected to three waves of Turkish rule. The first were the Seljuk Turks. They were a coalition of Central Asian tribes that accepted Islam and fought strenuously in the Middle East, both against other Muslims and against Christians in the Crusades. Their empire was established in 1037 CE and their leaders were in command until 1194 CE. They took control of the eastern Islamic world. The second Turkish rule was waged by the Mamluks from Egypt and the third by the Ottomans.

To summarise and make clearer the main events in Islam that have affected our narrative from the time ascribed to Muhammad's death up to modern times, the following list is appended (years are in CE):

632 Death of Muhammad
632-661 The Rashidun, the four Rightly Guided Ones (Abu Bakr, 'Umar, 'Uthman, 'Ali)
661-750 The Umayyad dynasty, ruled from Damascus
750-1258 The Abbasid dynasty, ruled from Baghdad
909-1171 The Fatimid dynasty, ruled from North Africa
1037-1492 North African Moors rule parts of Spain
1174-1260 The Ayyubid dynasty, first established under Saladin, ruled at first from Cairo
1254-1517 Mamluk rule in Egypt
1517-1922 Ottoman rule established under Selim I

We now need to fit further developments within Sunni Islam and Shia Islam into this historical framework.

The Twelvers

Most Shia followers belong to a group known as 'The Twelvers'. They count twelve leaders from 'Ali to Imam Zamram, the 'Leader of All Time'. The latter was a young boy who disappeared in Iraq in 878 CE. The Twelvers believe that one day he will reappear as The Mahdi or 'Guided One'. This form of Shia Islam is the state religion of modern Iran, reinstated by the Iranian Revolution of 1979. For Iranian Shi'ites, the Ayatollah or 'sign of Allah', an esteemed religious leader, is a temporary replacement of the Mahdi, until he returns in person.

The Alawis

In the ninth century CE, Ibn Nusayr, a Persian, founded a separate Shia Twelver group called the Alawis, or the 'followers of 'Ali'. Their religion has been maintained with great secrecy and its structure is hard for an outsider to understand. Although the Alawis regard themselves as constituting a sect of Shia Islam, most Muslims, Sunni and Shia, have seen them as heretical. There are elements similar to Christianity in Alawism, including a ritual that is very much like the Christian Eucharist, and they have a divine triad which at times takes on human form. The latest human form of this triad was, according to Alawite tradition, 'Ali, Muhammad and Salman the Persian.

Furthermore, in distinction from most other Muslims, the Alawis believe that, after death, souls can be reincarnated into new humans. A non-devout Alawi could return as an animal or as a Christian. The Alawis have been centred in Syria, although there are other substantial Alawite communities in Lebanon, Turkey and the Golan Heights. Today, the Alawis comprise about 10 to 15% of the Syrian population. The majority of the population are Sunnis.

Syria under Alawi governance has become one of the world's hot-spots. In 1970, the Minister of Defence in Syria, Hafez al-Assad, overthrew the government in a military coup. He was an Alawi. He declared himself President in 1971 and his al-Assad family has managed to control the political life of Syria from this time.

In 2011, in the context of Arab uprisings against entrenched authority or the 'Arab Spring', there was a revolution in Syria. This struggle continues.

Islamic State

We now come to the most dangerous conflict of the present day. This is the conflict between Islamic State and the West together with some Middle Eastern allies. Apart from its conflict with the West, Islamic State represents a violent fracture within Islam itself; indeed, most of its victims have been Muslims.

Islamic State only recently appeared on the Islamic scene. It is a breakaway division of Sunni Islam. After the removal of Saddam Hussein from power in Iraq in 2003, the forerunner of Islamic State pledged to join with the terrorist group, al-Qaeda, in opposing the

West and its influence. That link has been broken because al-Qaeda has maintained that Islamic State was too willful and intransigent. However, Islamic State's time came with the civil war in Syria, threatening to bring down al-Assad and the Alawis.

In 2014, Islamic State declared that it had established its own world-wide caliphate and that its leader, Abu Bakr al-Baghdadi, was the new Caliph. Thereby, it maintained that it had authority—religious, political, military – over all Muslims wherever they lived. As may have been expected, Muslim leaders and communities around the world have condemned this claim to a new Caliphate, and have also condemned the methods used by Islamic State to enforce their control of conquered territories.

Alawite control in Syria has spurred on Islamic State. It is savagely opposed to the al-Assad regime in Syria, to Alawism as well as to Shia Islam in general, as well as to any Sunni Muslims who tolerate these 'heretics'. Obviously Islamic State is also opposed to the 'West', seen principally as Jews and Christians. In short, Islamic State is a Sunni breakaway, determined to subdue Shia Islam and any world forces that might support it.

The sermons of Abu al-Baghdadi, an Iraqi Sunni cleric now declared Caliph by Islamic State, are full of vitriole about these divisions within Islam as well as between Islam (actually, his form of Islam) and the 'West'. This is based on an interpretation of *jihad* as an unrelenting war on infidels. It is a complex set of gripes and disputations, heavily built around a skewed theology that is very hard to identify or analyse unless one has a fairly sophisticated understanding of Islam, its history and its various theologies. It is because this knowledge is so absent in the West that the emergence of Islamic State seemed to come out of nowhere.

In fact, it did not come out of nowhere. Its origins have been there for a long time, including being mixed in with forces that, at various times have been most opposed to Western intervention in the Middle East but, at other times, seen by the West as part of the militia worthy of support in trying to overthrow a repressive government, most obviously in the case of al-Assad in Syria. The irony is that much of the Western intervention in these areas has actually helped unwittingly to form and strengthen Islamic State and turn it into the dreaded form it has taken in recent times. Indeed, had President Obama moved as strongly as was being threatened against al-Assad in 2013 when it was suspected that the latter was using chemical weapons, it would have been the biggest boost that Isamic State could have received. This shows how very complex matters are in the Middle East. Matters are rarely if ever straightforward and any intervention from the outside has to be done with great care. Among the objects of care, must be religious sensitivity to knowing who is with and/or opposed to whom within the tangled world of political Islam. Perhaps one of these days Western leaders will realise that they need good advice from well-equipped multifaith theologians before intruding into what they understand so badly.

Other Divisions in Islam

Apart from the Alawis, there were other groups best understood as Islamic breakaways, though not all Muslims would agree on their Islamic legitimacy. Much of the rationale for their claims relate to the issue concerning the founding imams. Other Shia groups, for instance, recognised seven or four leaders instead of twelve, and there are innumerable sub-groups, some of which we can now deal with.

The Zaidis, one sub-group, recognise only the first four imams and take their name from Zayd, the grandson of al-Husain. They are closer to the Sunnis than to Shia in some respects, especially in not acknowledging the infallibility of imams.

The Ismailis, or Seveners, are the ones who accept only seven imams. They claim that the seventh imam was a man called Isma'il, whom they allege was deposed unjustly by the Twelvers. They also recognise seven epochs of the world; each one has received its own particular manifestation of the divinity. There were also seven prophets: Adam, Noah, Ibrahim (Abraham), Musa (Moses), Issa (Jesus), Muhammad and Ishma'il.

Like most religions, Islam's history is one of division and multiple interpretations, so often, as above, premised on divine manifestations, alleged fulfilments of the essential promise pertaining to Islam. Hence, one of the more dominant and influential sects of Islam is that of the so-called Ahmadiyya Muslims, named after their 'messiah', Mirza Ahmed in the last few years of the nineteenth century. They believe that Ahmed was the 'one who was to come' in the fourteenth century of the Muslim calendar, that he himself had visions of Issa (Jesus) and that he has brought Islam to a point of accommodation with Christianity and other world forces, proper to Islam's true purpose. In this sense, Islam is the fulfilment of the Abrahamic promise and so Ahmadis (as they are called) see themselves as leading the reconciliation needed across all religious and non-religious traditions. They are naturally regarded as heretics by many mainstream Muslims, mainly for the suggestion that there could be a messianic or any other kind of revelation subsequent to that of the 'last and greatest Prophet', Muhammad. Ahmadis have often been the subject of persecution in Muslim states.

Accounting for the divisions within Islam is difficult. What often began as a political division invariably took on the guise of a religious split and, in turn, these divisions have given rise to the many forms of Islam that exist in the world today. Politics and religion, in this instance, become entangled and neither can be understood without the other.

Nonetheless, the major difference, and the one that probably helps to explain most about the internal splits that spill over into our newspapers, including much of what fuels the fanaticism of Islamic State, is the oldest one of all, that between Sunni and Shia Islam.

Notes

Further information on the divisions within Islam can be obtained in the encyclopaedias already cited. The following would also be helpful:

> Heinz, H (2007). *The Shi'ites: A short history*. Princeton, NJ: Markus Wiener Publishers.
> Momen, M (1985). *An introduction to Shi'i Islam: The history and doctrines of Twelver Shi'ism*. New Haven, CT: Yale University Press.
> Rubin, B (Ed), (2010). *Guide to Islamist movements*. Armonk, NY: ME Sharpe.
> Wollaston, A (2005). *The Sunnis and Shias*. Whitefish, MT: Kessinger Publishing,
> Material on Islamic State appears in the daily press and the content and context varies. For an introduction see the following:
> Charles River Editors (2014). *The Islamic State of Iraq and Syria: The history of ISIS/ISIL*. Charles River Press: @charlesriverpress.com
> Cockburn, P (2015). *The rise of Islamic State: ISIS and the new Sunni Revolution*. London and New York: Verso.

10
Distinctive Features of the *Ummah* of Islam

We have passed from the early period of the establishment of Islam in the Middle East to the Middle Ages period when division and consolidation both took place, and then to the later period when Turkish influence became significant for the spread of Islam.

With this background of division, we are at a point at which we can interrogate Islam as to why the Muslim community might see itself as pitted against the rest of the world. According to the Islamic foundation story, the *Ummah*, or community, of Islam had been established in Medina and then in Mecca by Muhammad. It had thereafter spread far from its original home. How did the *Ummah* come to define itself in this wider world?

This is a vital point if Islam is ever to be understood today.

Islam as God's Community and the Role of *Jihad*

In the first place, it must be stressed that Islam is a community, no matter how diverse its geographical locations or the cultural circumstances in which it finds itself. Islam had subjected the Arabian Peninsula and then the Middle East generally to its penetration. Some of the known world had become Muslim; the rest of their known world was not Muslim—it was largely Christian or Jewish and there were other smaller religious groupings.

Islam's early formula to describe this division of the world was: *dar ul-islam* (the sphere of Islam) and *dar ul-harb* (the sphere of war). The *dar ul-islam* would have a Muslim ruler, a Caliph, and the way of life within this sphere would be controlled by the *shari'ah*. The *dar ul-islam* had the obligation to expand into the *dar ul-harb*. When Islamic conquest took place, the inhabitants could either convert to Islam or, if they were Jews or Christians, they would be accepted as 'Peoples of the Book'. Thus, the *dar ul-harb* was transformed into an extension of the *dar ul-islam* by means of *jihad*. The very fact of the division imposed the obligation of *jihad* or 'striving', usually interpreted as a robust expansion of Islam, at times explicitly militant. This religious exclusivism became a cornerstone of Islamic religious culture, utilised in periods of political and social tension to galvanise general Islamic support.

There was a natural progression from the *Hijra* to Medina, the establishment there of the *Ummah* and the implementation of *jihad*. This progression brought about the distinction of *dar ul-islam* and *dar ul-harb*. However, while *jihad* explained to the Muslims their progress from the Middle East across North Africa to Spain, the victory of the Christian, Charles Martel, over the Muslim armies at the Battle of Tours in 732 CE seems to have brought about the realisation that *jihad* had limits. By the ninth century CE, *jihad* as a warlike tool took on a much less central role in the politics of Islam.

Subsequently, *jihad* has been interpreted within Islam as a state of personal striving (and this has been claimed to be its more original meaning) whereby individual Muslims declare war interiorly on their own lack of submission.

In any case, *jihad* is enshrined in the written canon of Islam and in the *shari'ah*. There are thirty-five references to it in the Qur'an. Some meanings are ambiguous, while others have an apparently quite militant meaning, some might even say a belligerent overtone. However, the Qur'an and the *hadiths* both refer to the other, non-belligerent *jihad*, the struggle to achieve an upright religious life despite the baser instincts of the human spirit. Further complicating any ease of interpretation, some Muslim scholars have maintained that the martial or warlike *jihad* can only be carried out by those who have first achieved the greater *jihad* of self-discipline.

It follows that any formula that includes *jihad* can be interpreted in a pacifist or belligerent way and in an exclusivist or a non-exclusivist way. In a context where Muslims seek to control others and establish an exclusivist *Ummah*, its belligerent interpretation has tended to come to the fore and inevitably has dominated the stereotype about *jihad*.

Both the *dar ul-islam* and the *dar ul-harb* exist within the world environment. Islam shared, influenced and perhaps inherited much of the common belief of Jews and Christians that humans were the rulers and maintainers of the world. For Islam, this world has been interpreted to be only a passing phenomenon. It would eventually disintegrate, and Allah had been described by Muhammad as the one to bring the world order to a conclusion. As a Judge, Allah would come on the future Day of Judgement and divide all humanity into the righteous and the wicked.

After the final destruction, the wicked would be consigned to *Jahannam* or 'The Fire'. The righteous would enjoy a very physical Paradise, but outside the domain of this world. At death, the body, designed solely for worldly purposes, would decompose and the soul alone would remain. The human body had never been of great interest to Muslims; its usefulness was only for this life and so it should be discarded at death. The soul, on the other hand, possessed the appropriate faculties for life in the world to come. The passage of the soul, into the worlds of either *Jahannam* or Paradise, is what is meant by the 'resurrection of the dead' for Muslims.

Even *Jahannam*, however, is not a permanent fixture. Muhammad spoke of a time when it would be emptied and when the torments of the wicked would have achieved their purpose of removing the evil tendencies of the wicked. A blessed total humanity would then adore Allah forever more. This is the importance of the *Ummah*; it represents in current time the eternal community of submission to Allah that will persist beyond the end of the world.

The Issue of Gender in the *Ummah*

Looking further at the human community of *dar ul-islam*, the relationship of male and female within its boundaries has always been a contentious issue (as it has been in Judaism and Christianity). There is certainly, in the Qur'an and the *hadiths*, an enlightened approach to women comparative to the times in which the *dar ul-islam* was first established. Islam banned female infanticide, gave women the right to inherit property and curbed polygamy to the extent that a husband must be limited to four wives, and could only undertake that limit on condition that he could treat them all equally.

The statements of the Qur'an on male and female statuses nonetheless propose the superiority of males.

> Men have authority over women because Allah has made the one superior to the other and because they spend out of their property to maintain them; good women are therefore obedient, guarding their unseen parts as Allah has guarded them; and as to those from whom you fear disobedience, admonish them, and leave them alone in their sleeping-places and beat them; then if they obey you, take no further action against them. Allah is High and Great.
>
> *Surah* 4:34

As clear as the text sounds, Muslim commentary explains it as giving males the responsibility of taking care of women, and that it is from this interpretation that male superiority and authority derive. However, it can be stated that there are four areas where the teachings of Islam in the Qur'an and the *hadiths* seem to Westerners to impinge on female equal rights.

First, whatever the case that the Muslim male must treat them all equally, he can have up to four wives, who may or may not be Muslim; the woman can only have one husband and he must be Muslim. Second, there is the matter of divorce. The Qur'an is clear that divorce is allowed but only as a last resort. However, a man can repudiate his wife by declaring his intention to divorce and then waiting three months, during which he repeats his repudiations, to ensure there is no pregnancy. It is also allowed for the man to divorce his wife by three repudiations and not wait for the three months. A wife divorcing her husband must have much more substantial grounds – such as desertion, physical abuse or impotence.

In the third place, while the Qur'an allows women to inherit property, they may only inherit one half of what male heirs receive in a particular settlement.

Fourthly, there is the contentious issue of female attire. The Qur'an made it very clear that women should not be exposed to public view, but there are no specific instructions as to how this should be accomplished. Many styles of female attire have exploited the vagueness of the Qur'an in this respect:

> And say to the believing women that they cast down their looks and guard their private parts and do not display their ornaments except what appears thereof, and let them wear their head-coverings over their bosoms, and not display their ornaments except to their husbands or their fathers, or the fathers of their husbands, or their sons, or the sons of their husbands, or their brothers, or their brothers' sons, or their sisters' sons, or their women, or those whom their right hands possess, or the male servants not having need [of women], or the children who have not attained knowledge of what is hidden of women; and let them not strike their feet so that what they hide of their ornaments may be known; and turn to Allah all of you, O believers, so that you may be successful.
>
> *Surah* 24:31

Various Muslim communities in different geographical settings have attempted to interpret the Qur'an by imposing different styles of female covering. The *hijab,* the more common form of Muslim female attire, covers the neck and head, leaving the face uncovered. The *niqab* is more extensive than the *hijab,* consisting of a veil covering not only the neck and head but also the face, usually leaving only an aperture for the eyes. The *burqa* goes further and covers the entire body from head to ground, leaving only a mesh opening to see through. The *chador* and *abaya* describe female garments that cover the shape of the body.

The wearing of the *niqab* and the *chador* which covers the entire body seems to have come into practice only after Islam made contact with the Byzantine Christian Greeks in Syria, Iraq and Persia. This was the way that these Christian women dressed. Later, Muslims saw it as a practical way of protecting their own women from strangers with evil intent, and to distinguish Muslim women from others.

Some of the dress codes above are limited to certain Muslim countries. For some Muslim women, the attire is not forced on them by male authority but by their own desire for religious and cultural identity. For an increasing number of female Muslims, especially those in the west or Western-influenced countries, particular attire is not an issue to which they feel bound at all.

The *shari'ah* has led Islam, males and females, into a mindset and behaviour pattern that can certainly distinguish them from all others. There was an Islamic *Ummah* set up in the world that was able to define itself and prescribe its activity. The question that comes from the past is this: Can Islam survive in a global world where the *dar ul-islam* can still be protected, but it might not be granted the right to social superiority?

To answer this, we need to explore again some aspects of the origins of Islam, to discriminate between some of the essential and accidental elements, and to re-prioritise these for a different, more global era. This is a task of increasing concern among Muslim and non-Muslim scholars and others.

Notes

On women and gender in Islam see:

> Ahmed, L (1992). *Women and gender in Islam: Historical roots of a modern debate*. New Haven, CT: Yale University Press.
> Ahmed, L (2006). Women and the rise of Islam. In M Kamrava (Ed), *The new voices of Islam: Reforming politics and modernity* (pp 177-200). New York: IB Tauris.
> Haddad, Y & Esposito, J (1998). *Islam, gender and social change*. Oxford: Oxford University Press.

Hirsi 'Ali, A (2006). *The caged virgin: A Muslim woman's cry for reason.* London: Free Press.
Hirsi 'Ali, A (2007). *Infidel: My life.* London: Free Press.
Hirsi 'Ali, A (2015). *Heretic.* Sydney: Flamingo.
Lovat, T (2012). The women's movement in modern Islam: Reflections on the revival of Islam's oldest issue. In T Lovat (Ed), *Women in Islam: Reflections on historical and contemporary research* (pp. 1-9). Dordrecht: Springer.
Mernissi, F (1975). *Beyond the veil.* Cambridge, MA: Schenkman Publishing Company.
Mernissi, F (2006). Muslim women and fundamentalism. In M. Kamrava (Ed), *The new voices of Islam: Reforming politics and modernity* (pp. 205-212). New York: IB Tauris.
Wadud, A (1999). *Qur'an and woman: Re-reading the sacred text from a woman's perspective.* New York: Oxford University Press.
Wadud, A (2006). *Inside the gender Jihad: Women's reform in Islam.* Oxford: Oneworld Publications.
Wadud, A (2006). Aishah's legacy: The struggle for women's rights within Islam. In M Kamrava (Ed), *The new voices of Islam: Reforming politics and modernity* (pp 201-204). New York: I.B. Tauris.

Specifically on Jihad see:

Cook, D. (2005). *Understanding Jihad.* Berkeley, CA: University of California Press.
Kabbani, H, Hendricks, H & Hendricks, A (2006). Jihad: A misunderstood concept from Islam. *The Muslim Magazine*, 16 August.

11
Recovering Early Principles and Reforms: an Interpretation

Even a scant review of the Islamic tradition, such as we have achieved, is enough to explain why it is that Islam is often associated with ideas of exclusivism and robust defence of itself, including the use of warlike ways when needed. This naturally fits the current image of Islam, at least for many observers in the West, as a religion with a violent disposition.

At the same time, we find at the heart of the Islamic cause, from its earliest days, an element that suggests the opposite and many will argue therefore that no religion is less appropriately used to justify intolerance, much less violence, than Islam. Tangibly, there is no religion that has such strong and explicit tenets regarding tolerance in its sacred text, and no religion which has such a strong track record of dealing with other religions and minority communities within its jurisdiction in such a positive way.

As we have seen, in the early Middle Ages, when such tolerance was far from the norm, Islam built model civilisations based on multi-culture and multi-belief. By and large, a Jew, Christian or even Hindu was better protected in most Caliphates of southern Spain or northern Africa and elsewhere than in any other foreign state. Sometimes these people were not even so protected in their own land, as violence between Eastern and Western European Christianity and between Jews and Christians could testify.

We need to examine this matter in more detail.

A Muslim theological Justification of Tolerance

In *Surah 17* of the Qur'an, we read:

> And tell my servants that they should speak in a most kindly manner even unto those who do not share their beliefs.

In *Surah 21*:

> We have not sent you except to be a provider of mercy and peace to all humankind,

In *Surah 53*:

> To you be your religion and to me be mine.

Meanwhile, in Abu Dawud's collection of *hadith*s, we find the Prophet of Islam quoted as saying:

> Beware! Whoever is cruel and hard on a non-Muslim minority, or curtails their rights, or burdens them with more than they can bear, or takes anything from them against their free will; I (Prophet Muhammad) will complain against that person on the Day of Judgment. (Dawud Sulaiman, 2015)

These are surely some of the strongest statements of intercultural and interfaith tolerance that we can read in any of the sacred texts of major religions. They are part of the most ancient and revered tradition of Islam and could not be plainer in their direction or their rebuke of the beliefs and practices of so-called radical Islam, yet it is the latter, rather than the tradition, that seems to dominate the popular image of Islam today. Clearly, the task for Muslims and for anyone who values the place of Islam in the development of civilisation is to recover the tradition in order to salvage the image and reality.

This tolerance was not accidental nor, as we have seen, was it part and parcel of ancient Arabic culture, for that culture had been as faction-ridden as any other in pre-Islamic times. The tolerance was practised, at least partly, because of the Muslim's strong belief that Islam truly was the fulfillment of God's ancient Promise (to Ibrahim, initially) that he would establish a model community in the midst of the nations. This would be a community that would reflect God's deep desire that humankind should live in peace and practise all forms of personal integrity and social justice. This would be the community that would show the rest of the world how to live well and under God. In many ways, Islam can claim to be one of the world's great experiments as a welfare state and a democracy, a claim which an important if unheralded portion of today's Muslim population sees as Islam's way out of the mire of its association with terrorism.

A modern Muslim writer with a strong following, the Tunisian Mohamed Talbi, highlights the clarity with which the Qur'an promotes the sibling relationship between Muslims, Jews and Christians. He puts the case that because they share in the Promise made to Abraham, they should be respected and accommodated by the new Islamic community. The Jew or Christian could share in the Promise, even if the institutions of Judaism and Christianity had both failed to do full justice to it.

For Muhammad, it was Islam that submitted most fully to the terms of the Promise and so it was fashioned around the concept that it was the nation that God had promised, the true 'People of God', or '*Ummah Wahida*'. Inspired by Moses (Musa) and Jesus (Issa), Muhammad went on to establish the religion that he believed both of them had striven to erect, albeit in vain. He therefore saw no contradiction in praising their efforts while showing up the failure of their institutional religions to follow authentically the terms of the Promise.

The way the story presents it, Muhammad seems quite clear that Ibrahim, Musa, Issa and he himself were at one in their vision and their adherence to the Promise. They were all prophets of God and he declares himself to be 'the last and greatest' only because he finally established the model community *(Ummah)* in the form of Islam. Muhammad is presented as one who sees his own prophetic status as part of a continuous heritage stretching from Ibrahim through Musa and Issa, the heritage being of muslims (submitters to God), including all the ancient prophets (as mentioned in the Hebrew Scriptures), as well as John the Baptist and Mary, mother of Issa, all of whom strove to do God's will.

In the same way, any Jew who lived by the Ten Commandments or any Christian who followed Jesus' Great Commandment (to love God and neighbour), was a 'muslim', and so to be respected and accommodated as such in the *Ummah*. By inference, the authentic followers of any religion could also be accommodated as being 'muslim', even though they didn't share the 'Peoples of the Book' heritage.

Importantly, Muhammad is presented as one who is determined to be tolerant of the followers of other religions because Allah himself has commanded it. In *Surah 17*, Allah is deemed to say:

> 'And tell my servants that they should speak in a most kindly manner even unto those who do not share their beliefs'.

In *Surah 53*, we read the words

> 'To you be your religion and to me be mine.'

Both of these can only be read as Qur'anic charters for religious tolerance. This tolerance was seen to have a sibling quality to it in the case of Jews and Christians who were declared by Islam to be (fellow) 'Peoples of the Book' and, as such, to be respected for their beliefs. For the era, this can only be seen as an unusual gesture of multicultural largesse and religious pluralism. Within the great Islamic Civilisation that went on to capture the hearts and minds of most of the Middle East and much of Europe, Africa and India, the concept of the *dhimmi* (protected people) communities was unique.

As was said earlier, the *dhimmi* communities were those minority groups that lived within an Islamic society but followed another religion. They were tolerated, respected and indeed often regarded as an indispensable contributor to the richness of the Islamic *Ummah*. For hundreds of years, generations of Jewish and Christian communities lived, and even prospered in many cases, within Islamic worlds as *dhimmi* communities.

Dhimmitude

We need to take this aspect of Islam further. There is much debate in the scholarly world about the merits and de-merits of what is sometimes called '*dhimmitude*' (a French term) in Islam (see Bat Ye'or, 2002; Lewis, 2002). Dhimmitude refers to the Islamic social ethic of showing fairness and justice to the minorities within Muslim boundaries. Some of the views one will find are more clearly based on an interpretation of the historical source material, while others are more clearly influenced by recent events. Our own interpretation is that, human frailty notwithstanding, *dhimmitude* in Islam deserves its reputation as a ground-breaking social attitude and practice, relative to its times.

The important thing to note about this Muslim social ethic was that it appeared to come directly from the early Muslim community's understanding of the will of Muhammad about matters of dealing with difference and especially minority communities. As such, the injunction regarding tolerance was based directly on Allah's injunctions and to be a defining feature of the model community, the *Ummah* that was established in Allah's name. To be Muslim was to be fair and to be just to minorities, in the way enjoined by God and interpreted by the prophets, finally by the last and greatest of these, Muhammad.

It is on the basis of this kind of evidence from the foundational sacred sources of Islam that we assert that, in spite of the stereotype and what might seem evidence to the contrary, no religion is more inappropriately branded as an instrument of intolerance, least of all violent intolerance, than Islam. One of the challenges for modern Islamic and other religious scholarship is in re-capturing the story of Islam as one of tolerance and social reform.

In this spirit, in the foreword to an influential book by Harun Yahya (2002), we read:

> Muslims must recapture the true spirit of Islam, and reclaim it from those who have harmed its integrity and honour ....
> (p13)

Yahya illustrates the point by using the core text of all Muslims, the holy Qur'an, to prove that true Islam cannot in any way, shape or form be associated with terrorism.

Interfaith Experiments

Similarly, the Muslim Mohamed Talbi's (1995) view of Islam as being most properly a leader of interfaith dialogue and reform, and his interpretation of the spirit of the Qur'an in impelling Islam in this direction, is clear:

> ...the dialogue with all men of all kinds of faiths and ideologies is from now and onwards strictly and irreversibly unavoidable. Man has never lived in isolation, and man's history may be considered as an irreversible process of an unceasingly extending communication. Man's fulfillment is in community and relationship. And this is written in the Qur'an! 'O mankind! We created you from a single (pair) of a male and a female, and made you into nations and tribes, that ye may know (be friendly towards) each other ...'

> . . . it is not impossible to admit the plurality of the paths of salvation, both in and outside the Islamic tradition providing people are both sincere and righteous. If this can be admitted . . . we can think of the whole of mankind as a brotherly 'community of communities'—or God's Family as the Hadith states—in which everyone has the right to be different, to be accepted, and fully respected in his chosen differences. To respect others in their chosen and assumed differences—not just to tolerate them on point of pain—is finally to respect God's Will Who willingly created man free to choose what he likes to be and to build with true liberty his own destiny... (And this is written in the Qur'an): 'Thou wilt not guide the one whom thou lovest; but God guides those whom He will. And He knows best those who are truly guided.'

> . . . For me, Dialogue is above all a mood, a spirit of openness, a disinteresting collaboration that does not challenge the presuppositions of the respective partners. We have to focus on cooperation in real and urgent issues confronting our human family, and the first step toward peaceful co-existence and cooperation among communities of different faiths and ideologies is to shy away from thinking in nationalistic or exclusive terms to believing in global and universal ones. We are, all of us, embarked on the same frail boat and, from now onwards, we can have only an interdependent future. (pp 61-67)

A Jewish scholar in Oxford, Ron Nettler (1999), in commenting on Talbi, says:

> The Qur'an, as basis and foundation of the whole structure, is Talbi's ultimate source. He sees in his theory of pluralism a 'modern' idea from the depths of revelation. Despite his obvious debt to modern thought, Talbi's point of departure is from within the sacred text and its early historical context. His approach to that text and history presupposes there is a humanistic message of the Golden Rule and an empirical validity in historical sources such as the Constitution of Medina which support that message. (p 106)

The Constitution of Medina

Nettler's reference to the Constitution of Medina refers to the charter that, according to the foundation story, governed the early *Ummah*, the model community established by Allah. As suggested above, this community, together with most Islamic civilisations of the early Middle Ages, were notable for their ethnic and religious tolerance. Similarly, other features that one associates with the modern welfare state and democracy, rather than with the modern stereotype of Islam, were in fact to be found in early Islamic civilisations. Among these features were those concerned with social welfare systems, education and healthcare schemes, and, as we saw above, many issues designed to promote the status of women. Almost a thousand years before the so-called Enlightenment in the West began the move towards these advances, they were being experimented with in early Islamic civilisations.

As with ethnic and religious tolerance, these other features of Islam were not there merely by chance. As the story presents it, Muhammad had taken to heart the message of the prophets in the Hebrew Scriptures that God did not want sacrifice and ritual but justice and mercy to flow like a river, and that his people should act justly, love tenderly and walk humbly (submissively) with their God. So, he wrote into the 'Five Pillars of Islam' (for him, the completion and fulfillment of the ethic of the Ten Commandments and the Great Commandment), a practical social welfare scheme of tithing that saw everyone giving a percentage of their goods to the community. This was symptomatic of the fact that the supreme ethic of the Muslim put as much store on practical charity, welfare and wellbeing as on obligations around prayer. For Muhammad, this would ensure that Islam could never stray into mere platitudes in the way that he believed both Judaism and Christianity had strayed.

In contrast with what he saw as the structural weaknesses of Judaism and Christianity, the fact of tithing within Islam being constructed as a religious requirement guaranteed that, from the earliest days, healthcare and social support were made available to all, including in most cases to the *dhimmi* communities. Similarly, education was considered crucial as a religious as well as a social duty. It is not surprising then that the first 'modern' university was an Islamic university, generally regarded as the one established in Cairo in the eleventh century CE, with another in Baghdad following closely behind.

Finally, as we saw above, the issue of women's rights in Islam is predictably the most controversial of the many features of modern revisionist scholarship in and about Islam (cf Ahmed, 1992; Haddad & Esposito, 1998; Armstrong, 2001; Lovat, 2012/1). What is probably less debatable is that the issue was taken up more seriously in early Islam than in any religious establishment before its time and that the early crafting of the *shari'ah* reflects this priority. The debate is more about the directionality of the attention that was given to the issue. Again, we side with essentially, though not exclusively, feminist Muslim scholarship that suggests that Islam represents a positive moment in the liberation and equality of women and that, as with its many other reforms, this came centuries before, and no doubt influenced, similar reforms in the West (Lovat, 2012/2).

This is perhaps a quite different approach to Islam than seen in popular Western awareness. Islam as violent, intolerant, anti-feminist, anti-social lies in diametric opposition to what has been stated above.

Notes

This chapter covers a wide expanse in the understanding of Islam. The following texts are grouped under headings and authors.

On the problems of tolerance with regard to Islam in particular, see:

Armstrong, K (2001). *The battle for God: Fundamentalism in Judaism, Christianity and Islam*. London: Harper Collins.
Crotty, R (2006). The first step before teaching religious tolerance. *Journal of Religious Education, 53*(3), 63-70.
Dawud Sulaiman, A (2015). Sunnah.com. Available at: http://sunnah.com/abudawud
Haddad, Y & Esposito, J (1998). *Islam, gender and social change*. Oxford: Oxford University Press.
Khadduri, M (2007). *War and peace in the Law of Islam*. Clark, NJ: Lawbook Excange
Lovat, T (2005). Educating about Islam and learning about self: An approach for our times. *Religious Education, 100*, 38-51.
Lovat, T (2012/1). Interfaith education and phenomenological method. In T van der Zee & T Lovat (Eds), *New perspectives on religious and spiritual education* (pp 87-100). Munster: Waxmann.
Lovat, T (2012/2). The women's movement in modern Islam: Reflections on the revival of Islam's oldest issue. In T Lovat (Ed), *Women in Islam: Reflections on historical and contemporary research* (pp 1-9). Dordrecht: Springer.
Lovat, T (2013). Sibling rivalry between Islam and the West: The problem lies within. In J Arthur & T Lovat (Eds), *The Routledge international handbook of education, religion and values* (pp 337-349). London: Routledge.

The more significant writings of Mohamed Talbi are as follows:

Talbi, M (1995). Unavoidable dialogue in a pluralist world: A personal account. *Encounters: Journal of Inter-cultural Perspectives, 1*(1), 56-69.
Talbi, M & Jarczyk, G (2002). *Penseur libre en islam*. Paris: Albin Michel.
Talbi, M (2002). *Universalité du Coran*. Arles: Actes Sud.

The writings of Ron Nettler at Oxford University are represented by:

Nettler, R (Ed), (1995). *Medieval and modern perspectives on Muslim-Jewish relations.* Oxford: Harwood Academic Publishers.

Nettler, R (1999). *Mohamed Talbi's theory of religious pluralism: A modernist Islamic outlook. The Maghreb Review,* 24 (3-4), 98-107.

Nettler, R (2000). Islam, politics and democracy: Mohamed Talbi and Islamic modernism. *The Political Quarterly,* 71, 50-59.

Some of the writings of Haroun Yahya can be found in:

Yahya, H (1999). *Perished nations.* London: Ta Ha Publishers.
Yahya, H (2002). *Islam denounces terrorism.* Bristol: Amal Press.

The concept of *dhimmitude* is explicitly covered in:

Bat Ye'or (2002). *Islam and dhimmitude: Where civilizations collide.* Madison, NJ: Associated Universities Presses.

12
Medieval Reform and Scholarship

Islam's contribution to reform and scholarship can be seen to have been present from its earliest days, or at least present in the stories about the foundations of Medina and Mecca. These foundation events however are, as we suggest above, not so much matters of historical record as parts of the important story that explains and sustains Islam. There is no independent verification for them and no physical evidence, written or archaeological, left to us. They nonetheless remain vital matters of faith.

In the case of the later Islamic communities that settled in other parts of northern Africa and southern Spain, it is different. Especially in the case of the so-called *Convivencia* ('harmonious co-existence') in the cities and regions of medieval southern Spain, we have plenty of historical reports and physical evidence that still survive relating to their ground-breaking civilisations. Some of these are close to a millennium ahead of similar developments during the so-called 'Enlightenment' in Christian Europe.

In these instances, Muslims shared their civilisation with other Jewish and Christian groups.

Islamic-Christian Interface

Cultural relations between Islam and Christian Europe occurred largely through Muslim peoples moving northwards into Spain, as well as Sicily and Naples. It was in Spain, especially, that Islam settled, dominated and developed from around 800 CE through until the end of the fifteenth century. In Toledo, in the mid-1100s CE, Archbishop Raymond, the Christian leader of the city, recognised the huge value to Christianity of the burgeoning scholarship of the Muslims surrounding him.

Toledo at the time was a Muslim Caliphate and so Raymond was acutely aware of the importance of the Christians in his care coming to understand the advanced culture of the Islam of the day. He encouraged dialogue and interfaith engagement of a variety of kinds, much of it quite beyond what would be considered the norm even today. Among many innovations, Raymond established a translation bureau with the specific task of translating key Islamic texts from Arabic into the language of the church, Latin.

In this way, the thought of great Muslim scholars like al-Farabi, Ibn Sina [Avicenna], and Ibn Rushd [Averroes] was conveyed to the West. As an essential part of this endeavour, the works of Aristotle, almost lost to the West but at the heart of most Islamic scholarship, were also translated into Latin, via Arabic from the original Greek. In the 100 years or so following, it was this translated Aristotle and the commentaries of the Muslim scholars that would have such a profound influence on the great Christian philosopher and theologian, Thomas Aquinas, whose scholarship would dominate much of Christianity's second millennium.

Islamic Scholarship's Influence on the West

As mentioned above, one key translation was of the work of Abu al-Farabi (872-950 CE, known popularly as Alpharabius), an outstanding Syrian mathematician, scientist, philosopher and musician. Like so many of the Muslim scholars of his time, he was what is referred to as a polymath (an expert in a number of fields). One way or another, most of his work sprang from the scholarship of Aristotle. Ironically, al-Farabi had been influenced by the Arabic translations of Greek philosophers by Nestorian Christians in Syria and Baghdad in earlier times.

It was these Arab Christians of the first few centuries of Christianity who had translated Aristotle from the Greek because they could see the huge value of his texts. However, the Nestorian Church, like so much of Arab Christianity, was declared 'heretical' by the Roman Church during the Councils of the fourth and fifth centuries CE. Councils such as Nicaea (325 CE), Chalcedon (451 CE) and, in the case of the Nestorians, Ephesus (431 CE) had progressively disenfranchised the more scholarly and monastic Arab Church for reasons partly theological but heavily political. It was in part this disenfranchising, and eventually splitting apart of Eastern and Western Christianity that had plunged the latter into the Dark Ages.

Aquinas was one of the architects of bringing Western Christianity out of the Dark Ages and the key for doing this was Islamic scholarship that rested so heavily on Aristotelianism. This was the same scholarly tool that had originally been preserved by a 'heretical' (to Rome) Arab Christianity. With Aquinas, things had come full circle but only thanks to the kind of work done earlier by al-Farabi.

As part of his philosophical work, al-Farabi renewed forms of Aristotelian logic, which would go on to form the basis of later Western philosophy's development of Formal Logic as a foundational sub-discipline of philosophy. Furthermore, al-Farabi placed emphasis on the ability of each person to discern and discriminate between good and evil on the basis of logic. The combination of this facility to discern the rights and wrongs of any human action, together with each person's free will, became the basis of a new form of moral thinking that, through Aquinas, would go on to challenge the old, less-empowering Augustinian morality. Aquinas's important concept of *synderesis* was of an inborn facility planted in each person by God that gave them the capacity to know the good as well as pursue it, and to avoid evil. It was based on Aristotelian natural law theory.

Aquinas's notion of *synderesis* amounts to a classic example of medieval neo-Aristotelianism and his debt to al-Farabi in this matter and others was direct and huge. al-Farabi earned the nickname, *Mallim-e-thani*, understood as 'second master (or teacher)', namely second to Aristotle who was considered the first master and teacher. His book, *Kitab Isha' al-'Ulum* ('The Book of the Enumeration of the

Sciences'), was adopted in Christian schools, just as it had been in Islamic schools, as an indispensable reference in a range of academic disciplines.

Roger Bacon (1214-1280 CE), the Franciscan scientist, made use of al-Farabi's ideas in his attempt to reconcile religious and scientific thought and to pioneer a distinctively Christian approach to science (Amin, 2007). Moreover, it seems that al-Farabi's book led to a revival in Arabic music in the very cosmopolitan atmosphere of Islamic Spain, as well as exercising great influence on Jewish thinkers who translated his works into Hebrew (Randel, 1976).

Another work that would go on to have a huge impact on drawing Christendom out of its intellectual 'dark age' was that of Abu Ibn Sina (980-1037 CE), a Persian polymath, known more popularly as Avicenna. Dominic Gundissalinus (known popularly as Gundisalvus, and a Christian convert from Judaism) was at some time in the mid-twelfth century CE, the head of the Toledo School of Translators set up by Archbishop Raymond. He was the chief translator into Latin of Avicenna's *al-Shifa* [The Book of Cure].

In this book, Avicenna has a chapter on the Soul, which Gundissalinus adopted as a Christian understanding of the soul as the substantial and immortal part of the human's spiritual nature. He also adopted from Avicenna the famous symbol known as 'the man suspended in space', a person with no relation to the outside world and yet his mind revealing to him that he is a thinking being who exists. The symbol of 'the man suspended in space' was mentioned by many authors of the Christian Middle Ages, and it is thought that Descartes in the seventeenth century most likely received it from them, going on to express the same thought in his famous assertion, *cogito ergo sum*, deemed to have heralded the birth of modern empiricism in the West.

Meanwhile, Gerard of Cremona, a twelfth century Italian who also worked in the Toledo School, translated *al-Qanun* (the Medical Canon) which became a text-book for medicine in European colleges from the thirteenth through to the seventeenth centuries. It was mainly through this book and its dominance of medical education in the West that Avicenna achieved such fame. In fact, in his *Paradiso*, Dante elevated him to a level alongside Hippocrates as a founder of medical science.

In medieval Islamic Spain, the philosophy of Abu Ibn Rushd (1126-1198 CE), the Spanish polymath known more popularly as Averroes, would inspire and direct the thoughts of the West in ways that led directly to the Renaissance, Reformation and Enlightenment (Urvoy, 1991).

It was Averroes who ultimately influenced Aquinas's most crucial works, including his central thinking on natural law. It was the stark clarity and purposeful intention of Averroes's rationalistic account of religious belief that so impressed Aquinas and, in turn, provided theological and religious belief with the philosophical strength that it needed in a world faced with the advance of science. On Ibn Rushd, Landau (1962) has the following to say:

> The western philosophers could have never reached the level we see today unless they had obtained the results of Ibn Rushd's research in philosophy. Muslim Spain has produced some of the brightest intellectual luminaries of the Middle Ages. One of them was Ibn Rushd … who is universally acknowledged as the great philosopher of Islam and one of the greatest of all times. George Sarton in his introduction to the history of science said that 'Averroes was great because of the tremendous stir he made in the minds of men for centuries. A history of Averroism would include, up to the end of the sixteenth-century, a period of four centuries which would perhaps deserve as much as any other to be called the Middle Ages, for it was the real transition between ancient and modern methods.' (p 32)

In turn, Averroes was himself inspired and partly mentored by another great Islamic philosopher of the day, Ibn Tufayl, also a native of Spain. Averroes reacted to what he saw as the over-reliance on the mystical thought of the likes of Abu al-Ghazali (1058-1111 CE), the Persian Sufi who also influenced Aquinas (Whittingham, 2011).

Whereas al-Ghazali had been responsible for much of the spiritual and mystical theology that solidified Islam as a religious rather than political movement, Averroes was intent on demonstrating that the heart of Islam could be justified in rationalistic terms. It was Ibn Tufayl's philosophy, especially as expressed in his most famous work, Hayy Ibn Yaqzan or 'Walk on' (an Islamic version of Robinson Crusoe), that convinced him that Islam was best understood as a common-sense formula for good living that could be understood by anyone who had the benefit of reason. Tufayl had conveyed this truth in simple story-like and poetic philosophies that were highly accessible to ordinary believers.

It was largely this element in Averroes that, in turn, convinced Aquinas that the essence of Christianity was also common-sense for the person with rational powers. For Aquinas, this was how he understood the Incarnation, God becoming human so God could be ascertained through nature, rather than merely through the strictly spiritual life.

Lastly, we must refer to the debt which Jewish philosophy owes to Muslim philosophy. Suffice it to say that Aristotle's works were not translated into Hebrew, but Jewish philosophers were content with what the Muslims wrote as summaries and commentaries and with the Latin texts. It was discovered by Western scholars that Jewish theologians followed in the steps of Muslim philosophers, and that thinkers before Maimonides owed their methods and ideas in religion to them. They also discovered that the work of the great Maimonides revealed beyond doubt the importance of a Muslim influence on Jewish thought.

Al-Farabi, Ibn Sina (Avicenna), Ibn Rushd (Averroes) and Ibn Tufayl represent a coherent, assured and persistent intellectual force in medieval times that went beyond anything the West could muster at the time. A great Western thinker of the ilk of Aquinas relied on this Islamic force to forge the reforms of Western intellectual life that represented his quest in life and his great contribution. He relied on them as much as on their Aristotelian underpinnings, for these Muslims were the ones who had taken Aristotle and applied his teaching to new and urgent circumstances.

There is little doubt that the understanding of Jews and Christians, and the entire West's self-understanding, would somehow be very different had these remarkable characters and their compelling ideology not existed. It would have been poorer. If one truly understands the intense sibling relationship between Islam, Judaism and Christianity, then the inspirational work of these medieval Muslim scholars on the West was entirely consistent with the origins and purpose of Islam in the minds of the early Muslims.

Notes

On Islam in the Middle Ages and its relationships with other cultures, see:

Fletcher R (1972). *Moorish Spain*. London: Weidenfeld & Nicolson.
Kogan, B (1985). *Averroes and the metaphysics of causation*. New York: SUNY Press.
Landau, R (1962). *The Arab heritage of western civilization*. New York: Arab Information Centre.
Menocal, M (2002). *The ornament of the world: How Muslims, Christians and Jews created a culture of tolerance in medieval Spain*. New York: Little, Brown & Co.
O'Shea, S (2006). *Sea of faith: Islam and Christianity in the medieval Mediterranean world*. New York: Walker & Company.
Randel, D (1976). Al-Farabi and the role of Arabic music theory in the Latin Middle Ages. *Journal of the American Musicological Society, 29*, 173-188.
Roth N (2002). *Conversos, inquisition and the expulsion of the Jews from Spain*. Madison, WN: University of Wisconsin Press.
Roth, N (1994). *Jews, Visigoths and Muslims in medieval Spain: Cooperation and conflict*. Leiden: Brill.
Urvoy, D (1991). *Ibn Rushed. Averroes*. New York: Routledge.
Whittingham, M (2011). *Al-Ghazali and the Qur'an: One book, many meanings*. London: Taylor & Francis.

13
Islam and The Wider Christian and Jewish Relationship

We now reverse the direction of our study.

A challenge for any Westerner who truly wants to understand Islam is not only to see through the common bias and stereotype to be found in Western commentary on it, but to go further and try and see the story from the Muslim perspective.

This chapter attempts to portray for the Westerner what Islam looks like from the inside for the typical Muslim believer, especially in terms of its foundational stories and beliefs.

Stepping into Muslim Shoes

A Jew or Christian wishing to truly understand Islam in a way that does justice to the tradition would attempt to study it from the Islamic rather than the more familiar, and inevitably biased, Christian and Jewish perspectives. The Jew or Christian would be asked, in so far as it is possible, to put on Islamic 'spectacles', to walk in Islamic 'shoes'.

We might begin with the common story of Ibrahim (Abraham) and his wife, Sarah, but temper the premise of the Jewish Genesis, Chapter 17, that Isaac was the heir to the promise, with the dominant Islamic view that Ishma'il (Ishmael) was the true heir.

The Jewish foundational story, which cannot be presumed to be historical, relates that Abraham and Sarah come into the land of Promise. They are promised that they will have possession of this land and a huge progeny. Sarah however proves to be barren. Abraham has a child, Ishmael, by a subsidiary wife Hagar and, only later, does he have a child, Isaac, by an aged Sarah.

Within this account (in Genesis 22:1-19), there is the horrific story of the near-sacrifice of Isaac by his father Abraham. Abraham was instructed by Yahweh, the God of Israel, to sacrifice his own son on an altar. He is willing to do so, but at the last moment his hand is stopped by an angel. The death of Isaac would have ended his hopes of a continuation of the legitimate line.

In pre-Christian times, Judaism focused on the obedience and faith of Abraham but, as the Christian era arrived, the Jewish tradition was more interested in Abraham's vicarious sacrifice of Isaac (only a near sacrifice, it needs to be said—since he was not really killed). Isaac became the symbol of Judaism itself. He had been (almost) martyred and suffered just as Jews were suffering in their colonial pain. He was the Jewish Martyr, par excellence (Crotty, 2012).

The Roman Christian tradition would eventually identify this Jewish Isaac with the sacrificed Jesus. Jesus, they claimed, was the New Isaac who had been actually sacrificed by his Father. There is a problem however with this extraordinary tale. When and why would this story of Abraham almost sacrificing his only son have been composed?

Foundation stories

At this early point, we must face a thorny problem. It deals with the position of Judaism in the above scenario of lands and ruling empires. Because of the close connection between the stories of Judaism and Islam, between the claims to the Promise of both and the conflicts that recent times have witnessed between the two, it is of great value to look further into the origins of the People of Israel.

Jews had (and still have) an established story about their foundation. They looked back to three great ancestors (Abraham, Isaac and Jacob) from whom had come the Twelve Tribes of Israel. To the ancestors, the divine Promise was given that they had inherited the land of Canaan. This was the same area that would be claimed by the Arabs as their land. The founders of the Twelve Tribes went down to Egypt and were threatened with extinction by the Egyptians. Only under a new leader, Moses, were they rescued and they attributed their escape in the Exodus out of Egypt to the High God, Yahweh, whom they encountered at Mount Sinai. The Exodus ended in the land of Promise.

The Jews claimed possession of the land that had been given to their forefathers and divided it among themselves. After two centuries or so, they established a monarchy under David and his son Solomon (the constructor of a first huge Temple in Jerusalem) which would eventually divide into two self-ruling kingdoms, Judah and Israel. However, these people would also undergo the throes of invasion from the same peoples also known to the Arabs—Egyptians, Assyrians, Babylonians, Persians, Greeks and Romans.

Following the destruction of Jerusalem by the Babylonians, the cream of the Jewish population was taken into exile in Mesopotamia in the sixth century BCE. They were allowed to return some forty years later when world domination had been won by the Persian Empire. However, the Persians would in turn succumb to the Greeks led by Alexander the Great and his generals in the third century BCE.

During the time of oppressive Greek rule, a family from Judah, later called the Hasmoneans, managed to muster an army and defeat a rather dispirited Greek army. They set themselves up in Jerusalem during the second century BCE and it was then that much of the consolidation of Jewish traditions and written texts, alleged to be about events from a much earlier time, took place.

How much of this supposed 'history' is history in the sense that we use the term? History has to be based on evidence. We do not have any independent evidence (apart from the Jewish sacred story) for the Exodus out of Egypt, the kingdom of David and Solomon, the two kingdoms of Judah and Israel, or most of what we read in the Hebrew Scriptures[3].

It would seem that we are not dealing with history, but with a recounting of an earlier Jewish 'world' by a much later one, in much the same way as suggested above about Islam. Where did the characters and events in these stories come from? The later Jews made use of the same traditions that were in the possession of the Arabs, weaving stories from them that constituted the sacred foundations of Judaism, just as the Arab people would do in the case of Islam. In fact, it would seem that the two traditions, Judaism and Islam, actually draw on the same heritage, namely of earlier Arab peoples in the Middle East.

Whatever the answer, we will not be assuming that the Hebrew Scriptures, any more than other sacred literatures, are relating history. The Jews had a well-constructed story and it meant, and still means, much to their culture and their ability to interpret life in the world. As we have seen, it is the same in the case of Islam.

What then of the Jewish god, Yahweh? Once more this will be contentious. Yahweh the High God, omnipresent and the sustainer of the cosmos, was not introduced into the Palestine area until at least the Persian period beginning in the late sixth century BCE (Niehr, 1990) and possibly later. In 586 BCE, Jerusalem had been destroyed by the Babylonian army but, in turn, the Babylonians themselves would succumb to the might of the Persians, a new force in the Middle East. The Persians required some sort of order and discipline in their newly-conquered lands. They sent emissaries, of unknown ethnic background, to Jerusalem and its surrounding area to accomplish this new order (Davies, 1991). Within the city of Jerusalem, the newcomers must have established the cult of this new High God, Yahweh.

There is an important, and possibly to some a disturbing, distinction to be made here. Previously, there was evidence of several cults in both Israel and Judah dedicated to the fertility and war god

---

3. See below p 118 for more on the contents of the Hebrew Scriptures.

of the same name, Yahweh. These cults would have existed side by side with other local deities such as the Canaanite 'El, Baal, Hadad and others. The earlier religion of this Yahweh can be reconstructed from archaeological remains and inscriptions at a few sites and in a few non-biblical texts. The local religion of the fertility god Yahweh appears as a normal development from Canaanite religion. Yahweh was another form of the Canaanite god 'El and he had a consort, Asherah. Any temple to Yahweh before the time of the Persian incursion would have been a temple to this Yahweh, a fertility and war god who had a consort, Asherah.

There were a number of other cults not dedicated to Yahweh (for example the worship of 'El himself, Ba'al and Hadad) in Judah and presumably in Jerusalem. 'El was known under a number of manifestations such as *magen 'abraham* (the Shield of Abraham); *'el roi* (God of Vision); *'el shaddai* (God of the steppes); *'el olam* (The Eternal God); *'elohim* (God). Whatever the case, this Yahweh of the earlier towns and villages was not the exclusive High God that came from the East, alleged to be the creator of heaven and earth. What in fact was the origin of this High God?

In this regard, the question of the rebuilding of the Second Temple of Yahweh in Jerusalem becomes important. There was a particular form of 'temple' promoted by the Persians, common in the Middle East. A temple was in ancient times not solely a religious foundation. It was an institution that linked landowners and official temple personnel with the king and ruling elite (Davies, 1992). This was the Temple built by Persian *fiat* in Jerusalem in the early sixth century BCE.

In fact, the Middle Eastern temple had followed a common religious form, combining architecture, personnel (both sacred and secular in our terms) and practice. Thus, it became the proprietor of public lands that were attributed to the deity as owner and it performed the function of a treasury for the maintenance of the god's city. The king held his position and power by appointment from the temple deity and his claim to public lands and financial income depended on the deity's benevolence. Hence, control of the temple meant control of the economy and regulation of the social structure, as well as supervision of religious ritual. Royalty and its administration and the priesthood and temple administration combined as the joint controllers of Middle Eastern society.

It would seem that the Second Jerusalem Temple, built by command of the Persians, was constructed hastily and without ornamentation. It was functional. By this stage, any remaining archaeological outline of a building or buildings, the so-called First Temple of Solomon, supposedly destroyed by the Babylonians together with most of Jerusalem some seventy years earlier, would have been conjectural. We have no idea of the First Temple's physical footprint, whether there was one temple or more, who were the gods of this temple or these temples or what ritual took place within its or their confines. However, the Second Temple was accepted as replacing an earlier magnificent First Temple of Yahweh built by Solomon.

What is being said here is that, prior to the incursion by the Persian forces, we are dealing with nomadic and partly settled peoples, of broadly-speaking Arab origins who had set up confederations in Palestine. There was no entity known as 'Judaism'. Characters such as Abraham, Isaac, Jacob, Moses, Joshua were Arab characters in ancient traditions.

The Society of Yehud

In short, Persia had a strategic policy that included the following: first, resettling peoples in new locations; next, either the building or restoration of temples for its own purposes; third, setting up a system of military defence, agriculture, taxation and administration based on the new or re-constituted temple; and, finally, the establishment of law-codes considered to have been provided by the temple deity. In the case of Jerusalem and its surrounding areas, this new entity become known by the Aramaic name, Yehud. It was the earlier Judah.

Perhaps, in Yehud by the end of the sixth century BCE, the economic and agricultural renewal was successfully underway, and this would have been followed by a military restructure in the mid-fifth century BCE. This renewal and restructuring would have been accompanied by some legal and constitutional establishment. The Law of the new High God Yahweh would have been compiled side by side with the economic and agricultural changes and corporate case law, some past law codes and new legal initiatives. All of this social activity had its centre in the so-called Second Temple of Yahweh. Nonetheless, this was still not Judaism.

The origin of the High God, Yahweh, is masked. The name (in this case 'Yahweh'[4]) could well have been borrowed from the fertility and war god known earlier in Palestine, but it was now applied to a very different type of god. Yahweh the High God, as an unattached male with no consort and sole creator of the world, was more similar to the High Gods in the lands east of Palestine—such as Sin (Akkadia), Marduk (Babylonia), Ahura Mazda (Persia) – than to the minor fertility and war god, Yahweh, known in earlier times in the Palestinian region.

The High God ideology had entered Palestine. There is no reason to think that the Arab semi-nomads had not imbibed it from the same source as the people of Judah. The people of Judah and the Arabs must have lighted on the notion of a High God together. In fact, there is no reason to think that the people of Judah were not Arabs.

The case can be made that what we later call the Hebrew Scriptures only began at this point. The traditions, set in place by the Persian scribes, had developed afterwards in Judah. They told stories of their Ancestors (Abraham, Isaac and Jacob), of their escape from Egypt under Moses in the Exodus, of their taking of the land once again, of their settlement and the structures of kingship and prophethood. Regardless, they were traditions collected and edited by the scribes of the newcomers, sent by Persia to control Yehud. The account of the stranger entering the land, and being given it by a Promise, was the means by which these newcomers validated their postion.

The newcomers, together with those who had never left Judah or Yehud, maintained these traditions. Then came the Greeks and, under the Hasmonean dynasty, these traditional stories became Sacred Scripture and Judaism began at that time.

Judaism made Isaac into the privileged son of Abraham, the Friend of Yahweh and the heir to the Promise. This privilege was normally reserved for the first-born. Was Isaac truly the first-born? The story went on to recount that Ishmael was dismissed and left the family of Abraham, together with his mother, Hagar.

---

4. Later Judaism would endeavour to explain the name of the High God Yahweh as 'I am who I am' *('ehyeh aser 'ehyeh)*.

If the Jew or Christian was reading this question seriously and openly, they might well be challenged by the inconsistency of this view with the text of Genesis, Chapter 16, wherein it is clear that Ishma'el was in fact the first-born, the product of Abraham and Hagar, deemed by the Hebrew Scriptures to have been a 'wife'. She had been introduced to Abraham as part of a deliberate plan to ensure an heir. So, it would seem, on the surface evidence from the Jewish-Christian sacred story itself, that the rightful heir to the Promise was Ishma'el.

This is the view endorsed in Islamic belief when Ibrahim returns to his 'first family' in Mecca and, together with Ishma'il, establishes Islam's most sacred site, the Ka'aba, on the very spot where Allah's creative work had begun (Hoyland, 2001; Rogerson, 2003; Lovat & Crotty, 2015). On the basis of this belief, it makes perfect sense that some of the earliest Muslims were known variously as Hagarians or Ishmaelites in order to capture that central belief that they were the true inheritors of God's promise to Abraham.

Seen from the Islamic perspective, the logic of the rest of the story makes sense. It makes sense that Musa (Moses) would be seen as the direct descendant of the 'Arab' Ishma'il, and that his separation from the pharaoh's house was essentially that of an insider, rather than an outsider, and that it was mainly owing to a rejection of the institutional religions of the pharaohs in favour of re-discovering the ancient Promise made to Ibrahim and Ishma'il. Furthermore, the wisdom of the Islamic position that the people who finally entered the Promised Land had rejected the spiritual interpretation of the Promise provided by Musa, in favour of the more tantalising institutional interpretation, can be understood.

It is a dominant Islamic view that the ancient kingdoms of Judah and Israel (whether historical or not) were established around a misreading of the nature of the Promise. The Promise was about establishing a people within a people, a people imbued with godly vision and godly ways, a people who would live and establish communities in ways distinctive of their beliefs. This was a vision consistent with their understanding of the *Ummah*. According to this Islamic view, Musa foresaw the rejection of the spiritual interpretation of the Promise, especially after the people's reaction to his Sinai message. The prophets, whose constant cry was against the institutional interpretation, also understood the Promise in this way.

We are unsure how the books of prophetic sayings came to be in Judaism. Possibly they were written in the centuries immediately before the Christian period as a critique of the institutional life that had shown itself. For example, the prophet, Amos, said the Lord does not want sacrifice and ritual but justice and mercy that flow like a river. Another prophet, Jeremiah, said the Lord does not want the Temple on the hill but the Temple built in the hearts of his people. Yet another, Micah, said that the proof of being God's Chosen was in acting justly, loving tenderly and walking humbly with their God. According to Christian and Islamic views, both John the Baptist and Issa (Jesus) held this same prophetic view, and suffered violent deaths for conforming their own actions to their prophetic knowledge.

Interestingly, the Qur'an offers a picture of Mary, Jesus' mother, as a prophetic type as well. It is yet another illustration of the richness that Christians can uncover in studying Islam that the Qur'anic Mary is so much more powerful and substantial a figure than to be found in the canonical gospels of the Christian Scriptures (Rogerson, 2003). Of course, there could well be a reason for this. As we saw above, many of the Christian forms and sources suppressed around the time of the Council of Nicaea (325 CE) related to a more human Jesus, to which many of the apocryphal sources were committed. The ideology that dominated thereafter was more heavily about the divine Jesus, for whom having an earthly mother was clearly somewhat enigmatic. Again, one of the great benefits of understanding Islam is that it has kept alive many of these earlier forms and their sources.[5]

The above Hebrew and Christian Scriptures' characters are all prophetic heroes in Islamic folklore and, of course, the supreme prophetic hero is Muhammad who, understanding keenly the spirituality that drove Judaism and Christianity, established the perfect religion to re-capture the essential spirituality of the ancient Ibrahimic tradition while rejecting the institutional forms it took in Judaism and Christianity

For Muhammad, the Five Pillars of Islam constituted, as we have seen, a dramatic re-statement of both the Ten Commandments in Judaism and the Great Commandment in early Christianity, but

---

5. As Christianity itself continues to mature and become less defensive, one would hope that Islamic sources of this type will prove to be of inestimable value in Christianity's own self-understanding.

were in the kind of practical form that could never be ignored by his followers in the way that Musa's and Issa's followers had ignored their central tenets. In Islamic folklore, living by the Five Pillars truly did impel the kind of communal living to which the Promise to Ibrahim, Musa and Issa had been directed. This communal living could be seen in the Islamic *Ummah,* that community that lived by the rule of God *(Hakimiyah Allah),* wherein social living was characterised by the prophetic virtues of the Promise, namely, justice, mercy and tolerance, as well as scholarship and spirituality.

Among those Muslims who know and understand their own broader tradition, there is a confidence that they relate more closely with both Musa and Issa than does the average Jew or Christian, respectively. For most Jews and Christians, faith and culture is wrapped up with their status as citizens of the so-called 'West'. For many Muslims, the 'West' connotes everything the prophets railed against, including at different times, wealth, opulence, imperialism and secularism. This stands in contrast to their understanding of Islam as being 'of the Promise', namely, God-centred, poor and humble, with Muslims often being victims, just as were the prophets before them.

Islam is often seen as the second huge branch of the Jewish trunk, although in a quite different way from Christianity (Nigosian, 2004). The connection between Judaism and Christianity is immediate. Jesus was a Jew who grew up, preached and enacted his sacred mission in the cultural and religious surroundings of Judaism in the land known then as Palestine. Muhammad is neither Jewish nor Christian, as the story goes. Furthermore, the context of the original Islam is in the Arabian Peninsula rather than Palestine, among a people for whom, by and large, Judaism and Christianity were minor players, at least in their most recognisable forms. In fact, as we have seen in earlier chapters, both Judaism and Christianity were present in the Arabian Peninsula but as virtual diaspora communities, separated from their mainstream forms.

For Judaism, this was how it had survived since the Fall of Jerusalem in 70 CE, as a scattered people and a fragmented religion that nonetheless continued to influence other peoples and religions through its intense and codified religious beliefs.

In contrast, Christianity's main survival form by the time of the official birth of Islam (622 CE) was as an imperial religion centred on Rome and Constantinople and controlled by the Byzantine emperors. This was the high age of Christian domination of the European world and indeed much of the world beyond. Nonetheless, the Christians who had survived in the Arabic world were largely displaced Christians, because of their many disagreements with Roman Imperial Christianity. As we have seen, Arabic Christianity had been among Christianity's strongest sites in the early centuries of its existence.

So, on the surface of it, Islam appears as a third major Abrahamic religion, a second branch, after Christianity, from the Jewish trunk. However, there is an increasing confidence in elements of Muslim and non-Muslim scholarship that there may be more to the story than this and that, indeed, the view that Islam actually emanates from much earlier religious forms that tap into ancient traditions with commonality with the Ibrahamic tradition are worthy of some attention.

The Muslim God

The central God-belief conveyed by the revelation given to the prototype Muslim, Muhammad, while similar to the Jewish Yahweh, discussed earlier, and the Christian Father, also displays awareness of an even deeper Arab tradition that there was a High God called *al-ilah*, 'The God' or Allah. From the above, we can see that, in part at least, this would seem to be the same tradition that underpins both that of Yahweh and Father. So, the traditional and Western favoured view that sees Islam merely coming at the tail end of the Jewish-Christian story may require considerable modification. Yahweh, The Father and Allah overlap as names for the High God of the deserts.

Indeed, many Muslim scholars and others would argue that it is in Islam where the conception of God as single, all-powerful, all creative and all-loving is perfected, partly they say because Islam emerged from a purer, less sullied and distracted understanding of *al-ilah*. That is, Islam was formed from the direct revelation and command of this High God, rather than through the more circuitous routes of the God of the Jews, who favoured one people over others, or the politically contaminated Trinity God of the Christians. In this regard, the Muslim God, Allah, perfects the God who wished to establish a people via the Abrahamic (Ibrahimic) Promise.

In parallel with Judaism, Islam relied on the same Promise that God made initially with Ibrahim, then through his son and heir (for most Muslims, this means Ishma'il rather than Ishaq/Isaac), reinforced through Musa (Moses) and thereon through the prophetic writings which constantly reminded the Jewish authorities that God wants mercy and justice rather than pomp and sacrifice. As we have seen, Muhammad identified himself as being in the line of the prophets (the last and greatest of them) and so Islam is rightly understood as the prophetic religion above all others.

In Islam, there was never a particular ethnic, political or religious eligibility required of the person who submits to Allah, who wanted to become Muslim. Allah was not an exclusive God but the veritable ground of all being. Anyone who recognises this, understands it and submits to God belongs thereafter to God's people. This denotes the nature of the *Ummah*; this is what Islam is. In this respect also, Islam can justifiably see itself as a superior form of the community of the Promise than the ethnically-bound Judaism or the politically compromised Christianity.

In terms of a relationship with Christianity, as we have seen, the main Christian feature that Islam has relied on has been the person of Issa (Jesus) himself. From the way the story is told, it would seem that Issa was the greatest prophet prior to Muhammad, described in places as the first prophet of Islam. As we have seen, Issa was a foundational prophetic character in the early development of Islam; hence, in the Qur'an and *hadiths*, one finds more reference to him than one finds in the Christian gospels (Khalidi, 2001).

As we have also seen, there is more about Mary, Jesus' mother, in the Qur'an than in the canonical Christian gospels. Does this underline the important influence that the older Abrahamic branch, Christianity, had on the younger one? Again, a case can be made that Islam has tapped into the many messianic stories and traditions that abounded in the centuries from the period of pre-Christian Judaism and the final writing up of the Islamic story in the ninth century CE. How many of these stories, captured by Islam in the form of Issa the prophet, pertained exclusively to Christianity's claims on Jesus or to wider shared traditions is another matter for ongoing scholarship.

Furthermore, to the extent that Christianity influenced Islam in this matter, which Christianity and which image of Jesus would it have been? By the seventh century CE, and more so by the ninth century CE, Christianity was divided politically and theologically. In terms of its theological divisions, none were more central than matters concerning the Trinity and the nature of Christ. If Christianity influenced Islam at all with regard to its devotion to Jesus, which Jesus was it?

If there is an answer, it would seem more plausible that it was the Jesus of the Arab church that, from a Roman Christian point of view, was heretical if not entirely aberrant. In that respect, Islam may have preserved elements of an original Christology that have been suppressed by Christianity's dominant Roman forms. Could it be that Islam might be a useful ally in Christianity sorting out some of its own theological divisions?

Even more tantalising is the idea that both Christianity and Islam have tapped into older messianic traditions that pre-date both of them, and that Jesus and Issa are merely compatible artefacts for the two religions. This would be consistent with the research above that illustrates the same common tradition flowing into Judaism and Islam. Whichever way further research takes these discussions, the important point to note here is that the relationship between the three religions is more complex than the simple view that Judaism is the oldest, Islam the newest and Christianity sits in the middle.

Regardless of these issues, the prophetic characters of Jesus and Issa remain points of commonality between Christianity and Islam with seemingly far more potential for mutual exploration than has been achieved in a millennium and a half (with the possible exception of the time of the *Convivencia* states in Spain and north Africa).

'The Christian Jesus and the Muslim Jesus' remains a largely untapped item of scholarship or popular dialogue between the two traditions.

We will now turn specifically to the Muslim Jesus.

Notes

Some of the material used in this chapter on the history of ancient Israel and its relationship to Jewish traditions and writings has been taken from:

>   Crotty R (2012). *Three revolutions. Three drastic changes in biblical interpretation.* Adelaide: ATF Press.

On the Isaac and Ishma'il issue, see:

>   Kaltner, J (1999). *Ishma'el instructs Isaac.* Collegeville, MN: Liturgical Press.

For explanations on the difference between Ancient Israel and the presentation of the story of Israel in the Hebrew Scriptures, see:

>   Davies, PR (1991). *Second Temple Studies 1: Persian period.* Sheffield, UK: JSOT Press.
>   Davies, PR (1992). *In search of 'Ancient Israel'.* London: Sheffield Academic Press.
>   Davies, PR (1998). *Scribes and schools. The canonisation of the Hebrew scriptures.* Louisville: Westminster John Knox Press.
>   Thompson, T (2000). *The Bible in history. How writers create a past.* London: Pimlico.
>   Thompson, T & Verenna, T (2012). *'Is this not the Carpenter?' The question of the historicity of the figure of Jesus.* Durham: Acumen Publishing.
>   Weinberg, J (1992). *The Citizen-Temple community.* Sheffield: JSOT Press.

On the technical question of High Gods in the pre-Christian period, see:

>   Niehr, H (1990). *Der höchste Gott: Alttestamentlicher JHWH-Glaube im Kontext syrisch-kanaanäischer Religion des 1 Jahrtausends vChr.* Berlin: De Gruyter.

14
The Muslim Jesus

The texts relating to the Muslim Jesus provide insight into the central role played by the Jesus religious hero in the early to mid-medieval development of Islam, a period when, by almost any impartial account, Islamic scholarship and spirituality were as open and vibrant as those of Christianity were closed. These were the dark ages of intellectual endeavour in the West, when virtually the only Christian scholarship happening was in the reclusive environment of the monastery while, at the same time, Islam was busy establishing universities with a measured charter of universal education.

Similarly, Christian spirituality was static and controlled by the papacy and its bureauracy whereas Islamic spirituality was alive and very much in the market place. The Muslim Jesus of the early to medieval Islamic establishment period, therefore, is likely to contain some strands of the Jesus tradition lost, ignored or expelled from the mainstream Christian tradition. This fact alone presents a compelling reason for those Westerners interested to understand their own history, including those committed Christians who wish to understand their faith, to make a study of this aspect of Islam.

This is quite apart from what they might learn about Islam itself.

Learning about Jesus from Islam

On the interior walls of the Dome of the Rock in Jerusalem there is an inscription on it that includes the following words from the Qur'an (19:33–35), words which are considered a blasphemy to Christians:

> 'So peace is upon me the day I was born, and the day I die, and the day I shall be raised alive!' Such is Jesus, son of Mary. It is a statement of truth, about which they [Christians] doubt. It is not befitting to [the majesty of] Allah that He should beget a son. Glory be to Him! When He determines a matter, He only says to it, 'Be', and it is.

Regardless of Islam's strenuous denial of Issa's divinity (or Muhammad's for that matter), Issa is a key prophetic figure in the early spirituality of Islam. In recent scholarship, he has been referred to as 'The Muslim Jesus'.

So, what is there to be learned from Islam about Jesus? Who is the Muslim Jesus, in contrast to the Jesus affirmed by the early church? The Christian Jesus was constructed not from historical sources but from traditions maintained in a broad and unsettled Jesus Tradition. Roman Christianity interpreted these traditions in one way, and the Roman gospel of Mark formalised them in one gospel statement. Mark was copied and extended, by Matthew and Luke, for constituencies outside Rome. John was entirely different. From a compendium of Gnostic writings, John's gospel was taken over by Roman Christian authorities and purged of its Gnosticism.

The eventual Christian Jesus was the Jesus of the Roman Christians: human and divine, born of the virgin, Mary, the Messiah who worked miracles, cured the sick, exorcised demons, raised the dead, was betrayed by Judas, was crucified as a bloody sacrifice for sin, was bodily resurrected and ascended into heaven. There is no need to see this Christian Jesus as more historical or more authentic than any other presentation, including the Muslim Jesus.

From the Qur'an itself, we find much of the Jesus Tradition with which Christians are familiar, like stories of a virgin birth and other miraculous events surrounding his birth. We also find elements in these birth stories that are familiar in much Christian folklore and in the apocryphal gospels, if not in its canonical gospels, such as the infant Jesus engaging in profound conversation with those who came to see him. Interestingly, many Christians will recall being told stories like this in their own infant religious education and Sunday school, even though there is nothing in the Christian canon, endorsed in the fourth century CE, to confirm such stories. A lot of them belong to the broadly apocryphal tradition, which was formally and ruthlessly discarded by the Roman Church in the fourth century CE, not always for the best theological reasons. The apocryphal tradition has been preserved in part through the texts of the Muslim Jesus.

We also find perspectives which might be quite challenging for many Christians, but which deserve some consideration, granted they probably reflect the kind of Christian thought about Issa that was said to be most influential for the early Muslims. While there is talk of his resurrection after his death, there is a very explicit rejection of Jesus' divinity, as we saw above.

The Christianity that, according to the foundation story, most influenced Muhammad would seem to have been at odds with the divinising of Jesus that was one of the central results of the Council of Nicaea in 325 CE. In contrast to the supreme blasphemy of suggesting that there could be another God or *shirk*, *Surah 19* of the Qur'an, cited above, makes it clear precisely who Jesus was, purportedly in Jesus' own words: he was a servant of Allah, a prophet, commanded to be steadfast in prayer, to be generous to the poor, to honour his mother and to be cleansed of vanity and wickedness. *Surah 19* tells us that was the entire truth and that nothing should be added (such as him being divine).

So it is that we find the Muslim Jesus to be what Khalidi (2001) describes as a 'controversial prophet'. While the Qur'an's depiction of any of the other Jewish prophets, including John the Baptist, is fairly much as we would expect from our biblical knowledge, the Muslim Jesus spends much time contradicting what many of his followers (i.e. the Christians) came to believe about him.

The Qur'anic account of Jesus includes what the Qur'an described as a 'cleansing' from the perverted beliefs of his followers. The Muslim Jesus engages in polemic, sets the record straight and is an active agent in his own 'cleansing' from being blasphemed by others who refer to him as God's son. The combination of this cleansing role with the demonstrable status of Jesus leaves one in little doubt that, at the heart of this heartfelt belief about Jesus' true nature, lies a strong Christian stream of thought, quite likely the Arab form of Christianity that had most influence on the early Muslims. Again, the geography and era would suggest this would have been the form of Arab Christianity rejected by Rome as heretical.

Regardless, the story tells us that, for Muhammad, the form of Christianity he came to know, with its image of Issa the prophet, was the authentic version, one that justified his own belief in Jesus as a prophet in the line of the Hebrew Scriptures' prophets. Roman Christianity was held to be in error, including in its thinking about Jesus. Through the Qur'an and the broader texts of the Muslim Gospel, Issa is given a voice again and, of course, we find him saying much of what can be found in the neglected apocryphal gospels, except that he says it even more strenuously. The intention to distance himself from the triumphalist and political Roman interpretation of his role is quite explicit. The texts related to the Muslim Jesus serve the purpose of giving Jesus the last word, and the authenticity of the triumphalist Christian church of the early Middle Ages (which would coin the phrase 'outside the Church, there is no salvation') is called into question by this last word.

There is much substance for reflection in the texts of the Muslim Jesus for a Westerner brought up to assume certain truths. This applies not only to religious truths, but the many truths about the entire Western Christian tradition that have originated from the religious assumptions of Judaism and Christianity. The Jesus to be found in Islam stands as religious, historical and cultural critic of much that we take for granted. The challenge is to reject the critique or to be moved to a new knowing of one's cultural heritage and so find oneself in a different place, including in a different relationship with Islam.

Notes

Further on the Muslim Jesus see:

> Khalidi, T.(2001). *The Muslim Jesus: Sayings and stories in Islamic literature.* Cambridge, MA: Harvard University Press.
> Ur Tahmin, A & Thomson, A (2002). *Jesus: Prophet of Islam.* Elmhurst, NY: Tahrike Tarsile Qur'an Inc.

On Roman Christianity see:

> Crotty, R(2015) *Peter the Rock. What the Roman Papacy was, and what it might become.* Melbourne: Spectrum Publications.

15
A Story of Loss and the Beginnings of the Troubles We Still Deal With Today

Why was the *Ummah* of the Golden Age of Islam destroyed? While medieval Muslims had a general understanding of their common ancestry with Jews and Christians, and the majority of Jews and Christians who lived within the Islamic world itself had come to appreciate their shared heritage, the Christian world more generally was ignorant of any such relationship.

These were the Dark Ages in the West, where education about anything was scarce and most Christians had little formal knowledge about their own religion, much less one as remote as Islam. What they thought they knew would have relied more on bigotry and superstition, so easily manipulated, than anything that could be called informed.

This ignorance provided the perfect grounding for Christian leaders, kings, queens and popes, to pull the exclusivist triggers of 'no salvation outside the church' and to announce the Christian 'destiny to rule in God's name' in order to wage what became known as the Christian Crusades (and later the Reconquista in Southern Spain, the wars waged by Christian Spain to re-take the Moorish south, Lovat & Crotty, 2015).

There were Crusades and Counter-Crusades. The memory of attack and counter-attack is seared into the psyche of all sides to this day.

This was the Abrahamic family at war in a bloody and mindless way for several centuries. The confrontation has left a fracture in the Abrahamic family unresolved to this day, and sitting behind so many of the world's most challenging issues, peace in Jerusalem and the rise of the so-called Islamic State being just two.

Many of today's global issues could be interpreted as a continuation of the Crusader conflict.

Crusades and Counter Crusades

Over two centuries in time and nine Crusades, followed up by the Spanish Reconquista, many of the great Islamic civilisations of medieval times in northern Africa, the Mediterranean and southern Europe were effectively destroyed. Along with the destruction went much of the Muslim credibility about Christianity (and to some extent about Judaism) that Muhammad, according to the foundation story, had extended to it.

Whole generations of Muslims came to see Christians in much the same way that many Westerners today would regard Al Qaeda and Islamic State, Boko Haram and al Shabaab, as artisans of mindless terror. Against their live experience of the worst kinds of barbarity that Christian civilisation could heap upon them, the kindly and equable sentiments about Christianity attributed to Muhammad became less and less believable. There are two points of immediate relevance to be made about the destruction of the original Islam.

First, there were consequences following the destruction of Islam that relate to its material prosperity. Beyond any religious considerations, the original Islam turned the world that it had rescued from backwater regions into some of the world's most prosperous areas. Islam served as a glue to pull together especially the Arab part of its civilisation. Out of the disparate and largely warring tribes of the pre-Islamic world, came a focus and a unity that not only spawned tolerance, social justice and creativity, remarkable for the times, but also wealth. Furthermore, it was a wealth that was largely shared among the people, courtesy of the Fourth Pillar about tithing and the principle of *dhimmitude*, in a way that would not characterise Western societies until well after the revolutions of the eighteenth and nineteenth centuries. Because Islamic civilisation was prosperous in this distributive sense, it became powerful in a way that only wealth distribution can achieve.

For the most part, Muslims believed in their Islamic world for reasons of both religious and social ideology. While Muslim reconstructionists like 'Ali as-Sulami and Nur ad-Din remind us that there was also an element of complacency in Islam that might be blamed for the disintegration of the original *Ummah*, the dominant Islamic interpretation nonetheless is that it was the external incursions of the Crusades and Reconquista that destroyed the Golden Age of Islam.

Second, the bloody treatment meted out to Islam through this time has left the seeds of profound resentment, rejection and a call for retribution. From there, it doesn't take much to have Islam's own exclusivist trigger pulled in a way that can be seen to justify as much violence as it takes to right a wrong, and to do it in God's name, just as the Christians did in this earlier period. This is the trigger of *jihad*, interpreted in a belligerent way.

It is a trigger that relates to Islam's claim to its rightful heritage as the completion of God's Promise to establish the *Ummah*, and to do so by reversing the violence done to it in earlier times by the infidel religions of Christianity and Judaism, effectively the spiritual foundations of the West. Deep in the psyche of Islam, this trigger has been pulled effectively in recent times, from the Iranian Revolution to the emergence of Islamic State.

Of course, the trigger does not come down solely to the confrontation of Islam versus the West, but it also relies on some of the deep unresolved tensions within Islam, dating back to its Sunni-Shia split in its earliest years.

The Re-establishment of Israel and Islamic Interpretations

Amidst the deep and long-standing suspicion by a portion of the Muslim population that the medieval Crusades represented an ongoing conspiracy on the part of the West to destroy Islam, the decision on the part of the international community to re-establish a nation called 'Israel' in the years immediately after the Second World War was a watershed event. At the time, the full meaning of the event was masked by an overwhelming sense of guilt and compassion on the part of many world leaders towards the events of the Holocaust and the attempted genocide of the Jewish people. The (largely Christian) West was left defenceless in its guilt.

While disowned and condemned by agencies such as the Nuremberg Trials, it was undeniable that one of their own Western Christian states had perpetrated the horrors of the Holocaust, using in part Christian, anti-Semitic theologies to justify it. The Third Reich had functioned largely as a pseudo-Christian regime, with a demonstrable level of complicity by the Christian churches which had too often turned a blind eye to some of the Reich's grosser atrocities. The sin against the decimated Jewish people had to be atoned for, and re-establishing their nationhood was seen as the ultimate political way of achieving this. The role of the USA, the UK and other European states in achieving this through the United Nations could not be overstated.

It was not the first time in 2,000 years that such a solution of establishing a Jewish state, preferably in Palestine, had been proposed. In the period between the two world wars it had been proposed with some enthusiasm. Even earlier on, in the later parts of the nineteenth century, there had been considerable migration of Jews to Palestine, especially coming out of Europe. This was a fairly direct result of growing European nationalism that had two effects on European Jews.

One effect of nationalism amounted to an early marginalising of Jews, such as would boil over into anti-Semitism some decades later. The other effect was seen in the renewed sense of the need for Jews to be reassembled in their own nation, to re-find their own culture. Moreover, there had always been a powerful lobby within American Jewry that had interpreted its religious heritage as necessitating the 're-building of the Temple' in the Holy Land of old.

At the same time, there was a growing concern in the Arab world that the desire, on the part of the West, to restore the ancient Jewish state had the potential to revive much of the odiousness attributed to the Crusades. Interestingly, the Jewish people were always divided among themselves about the desirability of re-establishing the physical nation of Israel. Many held that, religiously, the worst thing that had ever happened was the establishment of the physical kingdoms, legendary or real, in ancient times.

The Natarei Karta is an influential Jewish movement associated strongly with resistance to the re-establishment of a physical state for Jewish people. The Natarei Karta believes that the Promise to become God's Chosen People was not referring in any way to the establishment of a physical kingdom. The Chosen People was to be a people among other people, showing others by the way they lived what God's ways were about. While even in the United States there was opposition to the notion of re-establishing the new nation, opposition was even more prominent in the Jewish communities of the Middle East.

As suggested above, most Jewish communities living in what was largely a Muslim world were living reasonably well. The *dhimmi* Jewish communities of Islam had been treated far better than Jews had been treated in most of Europe. By and large, they were respected and, in many cases, even revered for the special part they had played in contributing to the original Islam. Many of these Jews had no desire to displace themselves from their ancestral homes to live together as Jews in what, for them, would be inevitably a difficult situation. It was knowledge of these tensions and mixed feelings, together with the practical concerns over who would be displaced to make way for such a nation that had led to a customary caution on the part of the international community towards any such solution. However, it was with the events of the Holocaust that the need to atone for the situation and to provide maximum protection for the Jewish people became an international imperative. At this time, the momentum for establishing an Israeli state became overwhelming.

There is rarely a solution to any problem that does not unveil another problem, and the case of the re-establishment of the Israeli state was no exception. Re-establishing the Jews meant displacing earlier inhabitants. It was not just the Palestinian Arabs, mostly Muslims, whose claims were overturned and whose lives were disrupted but, in many ways, the balance of the entire Arab world, already torn by the Crusades, Reconquista and later colonial interventions, was even more dramatically overturned by the establishment of Israel.

The single biggest upset was, nonetheless, the displacement of the Palestinian Muslim people. Into their place, and seen as invaders, came a largely foreign people drawn from the four corners of the earth, seen by them to have little tangible claims on a land that had been theirs for millennia. From an apparent solution, came at least one huge new problem.

In fact, the problems multiplied. As seen above, other than some early struggles and aberrations against the principle of *dhimmitude*, Jews had been incorporated fairly well into Islamic regimes. Unlike the cataclysmic confrontations with the Christians throughout the Crusades and down through the ages, there had been relatively few violent confrontations between Jews and Muslims. In a word, there was nothing threatening about the Jew as far as the Muslim was concerned, and much to feel grateful for among those Muslims who knew their history.

With the founding of the modern state of Israel, this all changed. For a start, 'Jew' quickly came to connote 'invader' or 'foreigner', well-backed with powerful friends in the infidel West. Additionally, because of the friends they were keeping, the Jews became associated with a Christian alliance in a far sharper way than would have been seen by the average Muslim in earlier times. The history of Jewish-Christian relations had been at least as strained as those between Muslims and Christians, arguably more so in the past few centuries and especially so during the time leading up to and including the Second World War. To have the alleged Christian West now championing the cause of the Jew and, in so doing, imposing what they could only see as a foreign Jewish state at the expense of the displacement of their own Arab and Muslim siblings was bound to change the perception of the Jew by the Muslim in a way that we are still dealing with today.

By the time of the 1967 War when the Israeli military, heavily backed and fortified by the West, all but destroyed the allied Arab forces (largely Islamic), the myth about 'the establishment of Israel amounting to a Western conspiracy to destroy Islam' had become a truth with any amount of evidence attached.

In the decades since that time, the evidence has simply continued to mount, if one is inclined to see things this way, with clear policy preference towards Israel's claims and against the Palestinian claims, on the part of most Western states and with countless violent interchanges that, for instance, have pitted a well-trained and supported Westernised Israeli military against stone-throwing Palestinians. In time, the futility of stone-throwing, together with the impossibility of assembling their own military, has led to new forms of aggression, such as kidnapping, hijacking, suicide-bombing and other forms of what has come to be known as terrorism. As often as not, this is referred to in Western commentary as 'Islamic terrorism', a language that, in the hands of the uninformed, amounts to a slur on all Muslim people.

The poor understanding of Islam by the West remains one of the major issues to be dealt with by Western politics, media and education. While it persists, things threaten to become worse. While it persists, an increasing portion of otherwise moderate Muslims are likely to be caught up in the aftermath of the exclusivist trigger pulled by so-called radical Islam, normally connoting the backbone of Islamic terrorism. Recovering some of the better times represented by the *Convivencia* states would seem to be a priority, noting that those states' harmony normally rested on the pragmatism of working for the common good, regardless of religious differences, as well as sufficient education about each other to ensure there were adequate bonds, in this case, familial bonds as 'Peoples of the Book', bound by a common Abrahamic tradition. Furthermore, the role of Islam as a leader of *Convivencia*, then and now, cannot be overlooked because it is the one of the three religions that possesses a theology of the other two.

Notes

For more on this content, particularly on *Convivencia*, we refer the reader once more to our other book:

> Lovat, T & Crotty, R (2015). *Reconciling Islam, Christianity and Judaism: Islam's special role in restoring Convivencia.* Heidelberg, Germany: Springer.

16
Conclusion

We have covered an enormous breadth of content in this study of Islam. We have examined the background of the Arab tribal situation and its surrounding peoples, some hostile and some friendly. We have charted the religious cultures of Judaism and Christianity which may have partly overlapped with those other peoples. Then, when dealing with the seventh century CE, we tried to understand the Islamic foundation story's coverage of the arrival of Muhammad and the establishment of Islam.

Thereafter, we have tried to follow the path of Islamic expansion, the core teachings and practices of Islam and Islam's reliance on the Qur'an, the divisions within the community of Islam and the dealings of Islam with its resident neighbours.

Finally, we have tried to chart the reasons, particularly the Crusader invasion, the Reconquista and the establishment of modern Israel, for the rejection by Islam of the Christian West and the rejection by Christians of Islam. We have seen that between Muslim and Jew, despite appearances to the contrary, there have been historically more irenic relationships, especially in the form of *Convivencia*. We have suggested that there is a need on the part of the West for education aimed at a better understanding of Islam. In particular, there is a need for Westerners to understand the cultural independence of the Islamic religion. In the end, we see no reason for the dire predicament that oppresses the modern world, namely that of 'Islam versus the West'.

The fact is that most Westerners know little about Islam. They know little about the Qur'an and its teachings, know little about the differences (and the causes for the differences) between Sunni and

Shia, know little about the Sufi movement, know little about the great educational, scientific and cultural achievements of Islam and know only a potted and biased history of the Crusades, the Reconquista and the establishment of modern Israel.

This dangerous ignorance has been the prime catalyst for writing this book, together with our earlier one referred to within the text. Both books have been intended to send the reader on a more objective search for information by education about Islam.

Looking back, what are the more salient features of the material in this book?

1. The Middle East was populated by many peoples. There were Egyptians, Mesopotamians, Philistines, Phoenicians, Assyrians, Babylonians, Persians, Greeks and Romans. At various times, one or other of these was in the ascendancy. On the fringes of these world powers, there were the Arabs. They have tended to be invisible in their recorded and unrecorded histories. Yet, they were there and they were very important.

2. The Arabs were mostly nomadic and semi-nomadic desert groups. From about 1000 BCE, they began to settle and became involved in agriculture and trade, but they maintained their tribal structures.

3. We have deliberately removed the Israelites from the list in 1. There is no historical evidence that 'Israel' or Judaism came onto the world scene before the few centuries immediately before the Christian period. In fact, there is plenty of evidence to suggest that those who became Judahites or Jews were originally part of the earlier Arab movements.

4. Arabs had access to long-standing traditions about Ibrahim/Abraham, Musa/Moses and later Isa/Jesus and many other religious characters related in traditions.

5. Arab religion was initially tribal, based on honour and tribal allegiance. The Arabs had many gods. However, at various times some of them turned to a High God, one who created all things and continued to rule all things. There was nothing unusual in this move. There were High Gods known among the Mesopotamians, and the Judahites later would accept the worship of the one god, Yahweh.

6. Christianity began as an offshoot of Judaism, breaking away by the end of the first century CE. Eventually, the Roman Christian Church overwhelmed other Jesus-movements (such as the Christians in Jerusalem, Arab Christians, Gnostic Christians) and the Roman Christian teaching and practice became normative. Christians also had one god, called The Father, who had been identified with the Jewish Yahweh. Consequently, the Arabs were mainly confronted with two separate religions: Judaism and Christianity.

7. Islam, via their foundation story's hero, Muhammad, did not see itself as a new religion. It saw itself as the renewal of a more original Arab religion, of which Judaism and Christianity were later and unfortunately distorted versions. The original religion was monotheistic, with its focus on The God or Allah, and proper to all peoples, including the Arabs, the Jews and the Christians.

8. Islam began therefore as a revivification of Arab monotheistic religion in the Arabian Peninsula and then spread towards the north, east and west. It established its own dynasties throughout the Middle East; some were aligned with Islam, some were less aligned with its religious culture. Islam was confronted with ire and conflict by both the Byzantine Christians and the Sassanian Empire in Persia.

9. Within the cultural worlds of education, art and architecture, philosophy, science, technology and medicine, the Muslim thinkers flourished. They established milestones in human intellectual achievement ahead of the West.

10. The most contentious event dividing the Christians and Islam was the launching of the Crusades. From the Christian point of view, the Crusades were waged at the behest of God, convoked by God's Vicar, The Pope, and charged with carrying out one of the most noble of Christian ventures: the reclaiming of the Holy Lands for Christians. From the Islamic side, the Crusades were seen as a barbarian invasion that wreaked wanton death and destruction. Up to this day, the Crusades have set up a barrier between Christianity and Islam.

11. There were times of *convivencia* (harmonious co-existence between the three Abrahamic religions) when Islam usually took the initiative and managed to live in peace and cooperation with

Jews, Christians or both. This was particularly realised in Spain during the later Middle Ages. The venture came to an end with the Reconquista.

12. However, there have always been 'triggers' within the religious systems of the three Abrahamic religions. 'Outside the church there is no salvation' is one trigger that has erupted into violence led by Christians, even in our own times; 'we are the Chosen People' is the claim that has led Jews to consider themselves above the common law and above cooperation with outsiders. For Islam, the trigger has been *jihad*. Although it can have a peaceful meaning (which can be said too of the Christian and Jewish triggers above), it can be interpreted in a belligerent way. In desperate times, Muslims have resorted to a belligerent interpretation.

13. Where do we go from here? This book is optimistic: *convivencia* was once realised in the world; it is possible that it can be realised again. However, it needs to be said yet again, that the great need is for education and the great enemy is ignorance. Islam must understand its own establishment as a universal religion. Judaism and Christianity must cease seeing Islam as a latecomer, a seventh century CE breakaway from them both, a usurper. There must be a renewed respect and tolerance of each of the Abrahamic religions for the others, and that will never be the case if the present state of ignorance persists. There is also a need for Islam to take a greater lead in establishing religious dialogue.

Some of the above points are very contentious. We have researched them and do not state them here lightly. We publish this book, with whatever faults it may have, in the hope that it will in some way contribute to deeper mutual understanding of the Abrahamic religions, to a renewed dialogue between them and, eventually, to attaining the goal of a restored *convivencia*.

Bibliography

Abun-Nasr, J (2007). *Muslim communities of Grace: The Sufi Brotherhoods in Islamic religious life*. London: Hurst.
Ahmed, L (1992). *Women and gender in Islam: Historical roots of a modern debate*. New Haven, CT: Yale University Press.
Ahmed, L (2006). Women and the rise of Islam. In M Kamrava (Ed.), *The new voices of Islam: Reforming politics and modernity* (pp 177-200). New York: IB Tauris.
al-Ghazali, A (1991). *The book of religious learnings*. New Delhi; Islamic Book Services.
Al-Tabari, M (various editors and translators, 1990). *The history of al-Tabari (The history of the prophets & kings—40 volumes)*. New York: SUNY Press.
Amin, O (2007). *Influence of Muslim philosophy on the West*. http://wwwrenaissancecompk/JunRefl2y3.html. (accessed 29 July 2014)
Arberry, AJ (1991). *Mystical poems of Rumi, Vols 1&2*. Chicago: University of Chicago Press.
Arkoun, M (1994). *Rethinking Islam: Common questions, uncommon answers, today*. Boulder, CA: Westview Press.
Arkoun, M (2002). *The unthought in contemporary Islamic thought*. London: Saqi Books.
Arkoun, M (2006). *Islam: To reform or to subvert*. London: Saqi Books.
Armstrong, K (1992). *Muhammad: A Biography of the Prophet*. San Francisco: Harper.
Armstrong, K (2000). *A history of God*. London: Vintage.
Armstrong, K (2001). *The battle for God: Fundamentalism in Judaism, Christianity and Islam*. London: Harper Collins.
Bat Ye'or (2002). *Islam and dhimmitude: Where civilizations collide*. Madison, NJ: Associated Universities Presses.
Bearman, P, Bianquis, Th, Bosworth, C ,Van Donzel E, Heinrichs, W et al, *Encyclopaedia of Islam* (2014). Muhammad sec ed, Leiden: Brill Online.

Bennett, C (1998). *In search of Muhammad*. London: Continuum International Publishing Group

Bornkamm, G (1960). *Jesus of Nazareth*. New York: Harper.

Brockopp, J (Ed), (2010). *The Cambridge companion to Muhammad*. London: Cambridge University Press.

Bultmann, R (1958, trans. 2005). *Myth and Christianity: An inquiry into the possibility of religion without myth*. New York: Noonday Press.

Charles River Editors (2014). *The Islamic State of Iraq and Syria: The history of ISIS/ISIL*, Charles River Press: @charlesriverpress.com

Chelkowski, P (Ed), (2010). *Eternal performance: Taziyah and other Shi'ite rituals*. Salt Lake City: Seagull Books.

Chilton, B & Evans C (Eds), (1994). *Studying the historical Jesus: Evaluations of the current state of research*. Leiden: Brill.

Cockburn, P (2015). *The rise of Islamic State: ISIS and the new Sunni Revolution*. London and New York: Verso.

Cook, D (2005). *Understanding Jihad*. Berkeley, CA: University of California Press.

Crossan, JD (1993). *The historical Jesus: The life of a Mediterranean Jewish peasant*. Melbourne: Collins Dove.

Crotty, R (1996). *The Jesus question: The historical search*. Melbourne: Harper-Collins.

Crotty, R (2006). The first step before teaching religious tolerance. *Journal of Religious Education, 53*(3), 63-70.

Crotty, R (2012). Hagar/Hajar, Muslim women and Islam: Reflections on the historical and theological ramifications of the story of Ishmael's mother. In T Lovat (Ed), *Women in Islam. Reflections on historical and contemporary research* (pp150-165). Dordrecht, NL: Springer.

Crotty, R (2013). The near-sacrifice of Isaac: Jewish and Christian perspectives. In A Cadwallader & P Trudinger (Eds), *Where the wild ox roams. Biblical esays in honor of Norman C Habel* (pp 192-209). Sheffield: Sheffield Phoenix Press.

Crotty, R (2015). *Peter the Rock. What the Roman Papacy was, and what it might become*. Melbourne: Spectrum Publications.

Dabashi, H (2011). *Shi'ism: A religion of protest*. Cambridge, MA: Harvard University Press.

Dahlén, A (2008). Sufi Islam. In P Clarke & P Beyer (Eds), *The world's religions: Continuities and transformations* (pp 678-695). New York: Routledge.

Davies, PR (1998). *Scribes and schools. The canonisation of the Hebrew Scriptures*. Louisville: Westminster John Knox Press.

Davies, PR (1991). *Second Temple Studies 1: Persian period*. Sheffield, UK: JSOT Press.

Davies, PR (1992). *In search of 'Ancient Israel'*. London: Sheffield Academic Press.
Donner, FM (1998). *Narratives of Islamic origins: The beginnings of Islamic historical writing*. Princeton, NJ: The Darwin Press.
Esposito, J (2004). *Islam, The straight path* (third ed). Oxford: Oxford University Press.
Esposito, J (sec ed 2011). *What everyone needs to know about Islam* (second ed). Oxford: Oxford University Press.
Esposito, J (third ed 2004), *Islam, the straight path*, Oxford: Oxford University Press.
Evans, C (1989). *Life of Jesus research: An annotated bibliography*. Leiden: Brill.
Fadiman, J & Frager, R (1997). *Rabia, essential Sufism*. Boulder: Shambhala.
Fitzmyer, J (2009). *The impact of the Dead Sea Scrolls*. New York: Paulist Press.
Fletcher R (1972). *Moorish Spain*. London: Weidenfeld and Nicolson.
Franzmann, M. (2001). *Jesus in the Nag Hammadi Writings*. Edinburgh: T & T Clark.
Franzmann, M. (2011). Gnostic portraits of Jesus. In D Burkett (Ed), *The Blackwell companion to Jesus* (pp. 160-175). London: Blackwell Publishing.
Golb, N (1995). *Who wrote the Dead Sea Scrolls? The search for the secret of Qumran*. London: BCA.
Grieve, P (2006). *Islam – history, faith and politics: The complete introduction*. London: Robinson.
Haddad, Y & Esposito, J (1998). *Islam, gender and social change*. Oxford: Oxford University Press.
Halm, H (2004). *Shi'ism*. Edinburgh: Edinburgh University Press.
Halm, H (2007). *The Shi'ites: A short history*. Princeton, NJ: Markus Wiener Publications.
Hirsi 'Ali, A (2006). *The caged virgin: A Muslim woman's cry for reason*. London: Free Press.
Hirsi 'Ali, A (2007). *Infidel: My life*. London: Free Press.
Hoyland, R (2001). *Arabia and the Arabs: From the Bronze Age to the coming of Islam*. London: Routledge.
Idries, S (1971). *The Sufis*. New York: Anchor Books.
Jenkins, P (2009). *The lost history of Christianity*. New York: Harper Collins.
Kabbani, H, Hendricks, H & Hendricks, A (2006). Jihad: A misunderstood concept from Islam. *The Muslim Magazine*, 16 August.
Kaltner, J (1999). *Ishma'el instructs Isaac*. Collegeville, MN: Liturgical Press.
Khadduri, M (2007). *War and peace in the Law of Islam*. Clark, NJ: Lawbook Exchange.

Khalidi, T (2001). *The Muslim Jesus: Sayings and stories in Islamic literature.* Cambridge, MA: Harvard University Press.

King, K. (2003). *What is Gnosticism?* Cambridge, MA: Harvard University Press.

Kluckhohn, C (1949). *Mirror for man: The relation of anthropology to modern life.* New York: Whittlesey House.

Kogan, B (1985). *Averroes and the metaphysics of causation.* New York: SUNY Press.

Landau, R (1962). *The Arab heritage of western civilization.* New York: Arab Information Centre.

Leaman, O (Ed), (2006). *The Qur'an: An encyclopaedia.* London: Routledge.

Lewis, B (2002). *The Arabs in history.* Oxford: Oxford University Press.

Lovat, T (2005). Educating about Islam and learning about self: An approach for our times. *Religious Education, 100*, 38-51.

Lovat, T (2005). The scriptural evidence of Islam: Ramifications for Judaism and Christianity. *Religious Education Journal of Australia, 21*, 3-11.

Lovat, T (2006). Interpreting the scriptures of Islam and implications for the West. *International Journal of the Humanities, 4*, 63-69.

Lovat, T (2006). Islam as the religion of 'fair go': An important lesson for Australian religious education. *Journal of Religious Education, 54*, 49-53.

Lovat, T (2010). Islam and ethics. In M Gray & S Webb (Eds), *Ethics and value perspectives in social work* (pp 298-314). London: Palgrave.

Lovat, T (2010). Improving relations with Islam through religious and values education. In K Engebretson, M de Souza, G Durka & L Gearon (Eds), *International handbook of inter-religious education* (pp 695-708). New York: Springer.

Lovat, T (2012/1). Interfaith education and phenomenological method. In T van der Zee & T Lovat (Eds), *New perspectives on religious and spiritual education* (pp 87-100). Munster: Waxmann.

Lovat, T (2012/2). The women's movement in modern Islam: Reflections on the revival of Islam's oldest issue. In T Lovat (Ed), *Women in Islam: Reflections on historical and contemporary research* (pp 1-9). Dordrecht, NL: Springer.

Lovat, T (2013). Sibling rivalry between Islam and the West: The problem lies within. In J. Arthur & T. Lovat (Eds.), *The Routledge international handbook of education, religion and values* (pp. 337-349). London: Routledge.

Lovat, T (2016). Islamic morality: Teaching to balance the record. *Journal of Moral Education, 45*(1), doi.org/10.1080/03057240.2015.1136601

Lovat, T, Clement, N, Dally, K & Toomey, R (2010). Addressing issues of religious difference through values education: An Islam instance. *Cambridge Journal of Education, 40*, 213-227.

Lovat, T & Crotty, R (2015). *Reconciling Islam, Christianity and Judaism: Islam's Special role in restoring Convivencia.* Heidelberg, Germany: Springer.

Lovat, T & Samarayi, I (2009). *The lost story of Islam: Recovery through theology, history and art.* Cologne: Lambert.

Lovat, T, Samarayi, I & Green, B (2013). Recovering the voice of women in Islam: Lessons for educators and others. In Z Gross, L Davies & K Diab (Eds), *Gender, religion and education in a chaotic postmodern world* (pp 173-184). Dordrecht, NL: Springer.

Martinez, FG & Tigchelaan, E (1997-8). *The Dead Sea Scrolls (two volumes).* Leiden: Brill.

Menocal, M (2002). *The ornament of the world: How Muslims, Christians and Jews created a culture of tolerance in medieval Spain.* New York: Little, Brown & Co.

Mernissi, F (1975). *Beyond the veil.* Cambridge, MA: Schenkman Publishing Company.

Mernissi, F (2006).Muslim women and fundamentalism' In M Kamrava (Ed), *The new voices of Islam: Reforming politics and modernity* (pp 205-212). New York: IB Tauris.

Momen, M (1985), *An introduction to Shi'i Islam: The history and doctrines of Twelver Shi'ism,* New Haven, CT: Yale University Press.

Nasr, S (2002). *The heart of Islam.* San Francisco: Harper.

Nasr, SH & Dabashi, H (1989). *Expectation of the Millennium: Shi'ism in history.* New York: SUNY Press.

Nettler, R (1999). *Mohamed Talbi's theory of religious pluralism: A modernist Islamic outlook.* The Maghreb Review, 24(3-4), 98-107.

Nettler, R (2000). Islam, politics and democracy: Mohamed Talbi and Islamic modernism. *The Political Quarterly, 71,* 50-59.

Nettler, R (Ed), (1995). *Medieval and modern perspectives on Muslim-Jewish relations.* Oxford: Harwood Academic Publishers.

Niehr, H (1990). *Der höchste Gott: Alttestamentlicher JHWH-Glaube im Kontext syrisch-kanaanäischer Religion des 1 Jahrtausends vChr* Berlin: De Gruyter.

Nigosian, SA (2004). *Islam: Its history, teaching, and practices.* Bloomington, IND: Indiana University Press.

O'Shea, S (2006). *Sea of faith: Islam and Christianity in the medieval Mediterranean world.* New York: Walker & Company.

Ohlig, KH & Puin, GR (Eds), (2009). *The hidden origins of Islam: New research into its early history.* New York: Prometheus Books.

Ozalp, M (2004). *101 questions you asked about Islam.* Sydney: Brandl & Schlesinger.

Pagels, E (1979). *The Gnostic Gospels.* London: Weidenfeld & Nicholson.

Pedry, A (2010). *Methods of Qur'anic analysis: A comparison of Islamic and Western.* http://www.suite101com/content/methods-of-quranic-analysis-a-comparison-of-islamic-and-western-a299353#ixzz1FmdTOqTf. (accessed 19 June 2013)
Peters, F (1994). *Muhammad and the origins of Islam.* New York: SUNY Press
Peters, F (2003). *Islam.* Princeton, NJ: Princeton University Press.
Peters, F (2004). *The children of Abraham.* Princeton, NJ: Princeton University Press.
Peters, F (1991). The quest of the historical Muhammad. *International Journal of Middle East Studies, 23*(3), 291-315.
Pew Research Center (2011). The future of the global Muslim population. *Pew Research Center: Religion and Public Life.* Available at: http://www.pewforum.org/2011/01/27/the-future-of-the-global-muslim-population/
Qutb, S (2009). *In the shade of the Qur'an* (vols 1-13). London: Islamic Foundation.
Qur'an quotations. The Koran Browse. Available at: http://quod.lib.umich.edu/k/koran/browse.html
Randel, D (1976). Al-Farabi and the role of Arabic music theory in the Latin Middle Ages. *Journal of the American Musicological Society, 29,*173-188.
Retsö, J (2003). *The Arabs in antiquity: Their history from the Assyrians to the Umayyads.* London: Routledge.
Robinson, J (1959). *New quest for the historical Jesus and other essays.* London: SCM.
Robinson, J (1990). *The Nag Hammadi Library.* (rev ed) San Francisco: HarperCollins.
Rogerson, B (2007). *The heirs of Muhammad: Islam's first century and the origins of the Sunni Shia split.* New York: Overlook Press.
Roth N (2002). *Conversos, inquisition and the expulsion of the Jews from Spain.* Madison, WN: University of Wisconsin Press.
Roth, N (1994). *Jews, Visigoths and Muslims in medieval Spain: Cooperation and conflict.* Leiden: Brill.
Rubin, B (Ed), (2010). *Guide to Islamist movements.* Armonk, NY: ME Sharpe.
Sanders, E (1985). *Jesus and Judaism.* Philadelphia: Fortress.
Sardar, Z (2006). *What do Muslims believe?* London: Granta.
Schimmel, A (1983). *Mystical dimensions of Islam.* Chapel Hill, NC: University of North Carolina Press.
Shanks, H (1992). *Understanding the Dead Sea Scrolls.* New York: Random House.
Shatzmiller, M & Hoyland, R (2001). *Arabia and the Arabs: From the Bronse Age to the coming of Islam.* London: Routledge.

Shoemaker, S (2001). *The death of a Prophet: The end of Muhammad's life and the beginnings of Islam*. Philadelphia: University of Pennsylvania Press.

Talbi, M & Jarczyk, G (2002). *Penseur libre en islam*. Paris: Albin Michel.

Talbi, M (1995). Unavoidable dialogue in a pluralist world: A personal account. *Encounters: Journal of Inter-cultural Perspectives*, 1(1), 56-69.

Talbi, M (2002). *Universalité du Coran*. Arles: Actes Sud,

Thompson, T & Verenna, T (2012). *'Is this not the Carpenter?' The question of the historicity of the figure of Jesus*. Durham: Acumen Publishing.

Thompson, T (2000). *The Bible in history. How writers create a past*. London: Pimlico

Ur Tahmin, A & Thomson, A (2002). *Jesus: Prophet of Islam*. Elmhurst, NY: Tahrike Tarsile Qur'an Inc.

Urvoy, D (1991). *Ibn Rushed. Averroes*. New York: Routledge.

Vanderkam, J (2010). *The Dead Sea Scrolls today*. Grand Rapids: William B Eerdemans.

Vermes, G (1997). *The complete Dead Sea Scrolls in English (complete edition)*. London: Allen Lane Penguin.

Wadud, A (1999). *Qur'an and woman: Re-reading the sacred text from a woman's perspective*. New York: Oxford University Press.

Wadud, A (2006). Aishah's legacy: The struggle for women's rights within Islam. In M Kamrava (Ed), *The new voices of Islam: Reforming politics and modernity* (pp 201-204). New York: IB Tauris.

Wadud, A (2006). *Inside the gender Jihad: Women's reform in Islam*. Oxford: Oneworld Publications.

Warraq, I (1998). *The origins of the Qur'an*. New York: Prometheus Books.

Watt WM (1974). *Muhammad: Prophet and statesman*. Oxford: Oxford University Press

Watt, WM (1953). *Muhammad at Mecca*. Oxford: Clarendon Press.

Weinberg, J (1992). *The Citizen-Temple community*. Sheffield: JSOT Press.

Whittingham, M (2011). *Al-Ghazali and the Qur'an: One book, many meanings*. London: Taylor and Francis.

Wollaston, A (2005). *The Sunnis and Shias*. Whitefish, MT: Kessinger Publishing.

Yahya, H (1999). *Perished nations*. London: Ta Ha Publishers.

Yahya, H (2002). *Islam denounces terrorism*. Bristol: Amal Press.

Zeitlin, I (2007). *The historical Muhammad*. New York: John Wiley & Sons.

Milton Keynes UK
Ingram Content Group UK Ltd.
UKHW012122021123
431722UK00004B/70